IGCSE
Study Guide
for First Language English

IGCSE
Study Guide

for First Language English

Julia Hubbard
John Reynolds

HODDER
EDUCATION
AN HACHETTE UK COMPANY

The Publishers would like to thank the following for permission to reproduce copyright material:

Photo credits: p.22 © Tibor Bognár/Corbis
Acknowledgements: pp.3–4 *A noise so terrible it makes you sick* © The New York Times Company;
pp.5–6 *Life on Inishmaan* Reproduced by permission of the University of Cambridge Local
Examinations Syndicate; **pp.12–13** Extract from *You Are Now Entering the Human Heart* © The Janet
Frame Literary Trust, the story first appeared in *You Are Now Entering the Human Heart: Stories*.
Victoria University Press, Wellington, New Zealand, 1983, reprinted 2005; **pp.15–16** Extract from
Rebecca by Daphne du Maurier, Reproduced with permission of Curtis Brown Ltd., on behalf of
The Chichester Partnership © The Chichester Partnership; **pp.19–20** Adapted letter from The Croft
Community reproduced with permission from The Camphill Village Trust; **p.22** *Romantic Riga* ©
Telegraph Group Limited (2003); **pp.23–4** *Patchara's diary* and *Programme* Reproduced by permission
of the University of Cambridge Local Examinations Syndicate; **p.28** Extract from *The Fury* © 1961
by Stan Barstow; **pp.31–2** *When the chips are down* © Nigel Baker, from *The Teacher* Magazine;
pp.33–4 *Alive: A gap in your life?* by Claire Sawers, freelance journalist and feature writer; **pp.36–7**
Text from the BBC News website: www.bbc.co.uk/news; **pp.37–8** *Beat the quake, man* Reprinted
by kind permission of the New Internationalist © New Internationalist www.newint.org; **pp.41–2**
All rise, here comes the judge Greenwood Communications AB, Sweden; **pp.42–3** *No ordinary seamen*
Times Newspapers Limited

The following questions from IGCSE First Langauge English examination papers and answer guides
are reproduced by permission of the University of Cambridge Local Examinations Syndicate.

p.6 q.4: 2005 J Paper 2, q.2; **p.13**: Reading task answer guide; **p.24**: 2005 J Paper 3, q.1 (section 1);
p.39: Summary writing task answer guide; **p.43**: 2003 N Paper 2, q.1a, 1b; **p.44**: Summary writing
task answer guide; **pp.73–5**: Composition task answer guide; **pp.84–5**: Speaking and listening task
answer guide

J = June examination paper, N = November examination paper

Every effort has been made to trace all copyright holders, but if any have been inadvertently
overlooked the Publishers will be pleased to make the necessary arrangements at the first
opportunity.

Orders: please contact Bookpoint Ltd, 130 Milton Park, Abingdon, Oxon OX14 4SB. Telephone:
(44) 01235 827720. Fax: (44) 01235 400454. Lines are open 9.00–5.00, Monday to Saturday, with a
24-hour message answering service. Visit our website at www.hoddereducation.co.uk

© Julia Hubbard and John Reynolds 2005
First published in 2005 by
Hodder Education,
An Hachette UK Company,
338 Euston Road
London NW1 3BH

Impression number   10 9
Year   2012

Cover photo John Townson/Creation
Cartoons by Richard Duszczak
Typeset in Bembo 12/14 by Pantek Arts Ltd, Maidstone, Kent
Printed and bound in Great Britain by CPI Group (UK) Ltd, Croydon, CR0 4YY

A catalogue record for this title is available from the British Library

ISBN: 978 0 7195 7900 4

Contents

Introduction

What is IGCSE First Language English?

IGCSE First Language English is an examination provided for students in international schools by the University of Cambridge International Examinations in the UK. It is targeted at students in the eleventh grade in their schools and provides a qualification which is recognised as providing evidence of competence in English for students who wish to study at universities in English-speaking countries.

Students' examination papers are marked in the UK by experienced examiners in order to ensure comparability of standards across the world and to validate the award of a CIE approved certificate.

IGCSE First Language English can be taken by students at either Core or Extended levels. It is expected that all students entering the examination, regardless of level, should use English regularly in both speaking and writing; it is important to remember that the difference between the Core and Extended papers lies in the difficulty and complexity of the reading passages and the questions.

What does the examination consist of?

The examination tests both reading and writing skills. There is one compulsory paper which tests both reading and writing at either Core or Extended level (both worth 50 per cent) and then there is the option of taking an externally marked paper which tests directed writing and composition or of submitting a coursework portfolio containing different types of writing tasks. Each of these components (the Composition paper and coursework) is worth 50 per cent of the whole examination. There is also the opportunity to take one of two optional speaking and listening components, which does not count towards the final assessment.

Component 1 (Core)

This paper lasts 1 hour 45 minutes. You will have to read one passage of 700–800 words and then answer questions which will test your understanding of it. Question 1, which will be worth a total of 30 marks, will contain a number of shorter questions requiring answers of different lengths. One of the questions will require the writing of a brief summary and will be worth 7 of the 30 marks available.

Question 2 will be a directed writing task based on the material in the reading passage. It will be marked out of a total of 20 marks (10 for reading and 10 for writing).

Component 2 (Extended)

This paper lasts 2 hours. You will have to read two passages, each of 600–700 words in length; there will be a common theme to the passages but they may be different types of writing (for example fiction and non-fiction). Question 1 may be sub-divided and will test your understanding of **Passage 1 only**. Question 1 is worth a total of 20 marks: 15 marks will be awarded for reading skills and 5 marks for writing.

Question 2, which is worth 10 marks, will also be based on **Passage 1 only** and will test your understanding of how writers achieve their effects.

Question 3 may also be sub-divided and will require you to write a summary of some of the points included in **both** passages. This is worth a total of 20 marks (15 for reading and 5 for writing).

Component 3 (Core and Extended)

This paper, which is the alternative to the coursework component, lasts 2 hours. It tests both directed writing and composition skills. It is divided into two sections. Section 1 is worth 25 marks (15 for writing and 10 for reading) and consists of a directed writing task based on one or more short texts printed on the question paper. You will be required to use and develop the given information in another form.

Section 2 is the composition task. You will be offered a choice of essay titles covering a range of different writing genres (such as descriptive or argumentative). You must write on only **one** of them and you are advised to write 350–450 words. The composition will be marked out of a total of 25. This comprises two different marks: a maximum of 12 marks will be available for style and accuracy and a maximum of 13 marks for content and structure.

Component 4 (Coursework)

The coursework option is the alternative to component 3 and is worth 50 marks in total. You are required to submit a coursework portfolio comprising **three** assignments each of 500–800 words; these should consist of:

- a piece of informative, analytical and/or argumentative writing
- a piece of imaginative, descriptive and/or narrative writing
- a response to a text or texts chosen by your Centre. Your response should show the ability to analyse and evaluate the material presented in the texts.

You must include the first draft of **one** of these three assignments as part of your portfolio. Work may be word-processed. A mark, out of a maximum of 40, will be awarded for the quality of writing. This is assessed across all three assignments. A further mark, out of a maximum of 10, will be awarded for reading, based on the candidate's performance in Assignment 3.

Components 5 and 6

These are optional speaking and listening components and allow you to exhibit your skills in this area in different ways. Component 5 requires you to give an individual presentation lasting 3–4 minutes which will then develop into a conversation/discussion with the teacher/examiner.

Component 6 allows your speaking and listening skills to be assessed through three different tasks undertaken throughout your IGCSE course. These will consist of an individual activity, a pair-based activity and a group activity.

How this Study Guide can help you

This Study Guide has been written by experienced senior examiners. It contains examples of the different tasks required by the examination and provides you with examples of candidates' responses to them. It also gives you details about how the questions are marked and what examiners are especially looking for in answers of different levels (**Answer guides**). There are exercises to help you improve your skills and specimen questions for you to practise. Throughout the Guide you will find sections containing **Examiners' tips** and suggestions as to how to prepare yourself for success in the examination. The Guide can be used to help you to prepare for the examination in your own time and is a valuable supplement to the work that you will be doing as part of your course at school.

TOPIC 1 Reading skills

Key objectives

- To introduce the key terms used to define the skills tested in the reading component of IGCSE First Language English
- To define the key skills/ideas involved in the reading component of IGCSE First Language English

Key definitions

These are the key terms that define what you need to be able to do in order to approach the reading component of the IGCSE First Language English examination.

Term	Definition
Understand	To grasp the meaning of
Explain	To make the meaning clear
Implicit	A meaning that is meant but not clearly expressed or stated
Select	To choose; to pick out
Collate	To arrange in order; to put together
Analyse	To examine carefully; to determine why something has happened
Evaluate	To consider value or worth
Writer's effect	The effect on the reader created by an author's words

Key ideas

Once you understand what the above terms involve you can read the syllabus objectives for your IGCSE course and create a checklist for yourself which sums up the key aims of the IGCSE First Language English reading component.

Here is a possible checklist:

- Do you understand what you have read?
- Can you re-tell or explain information that you have read, using your own words?
- Can you pick out details and information that is relevant for a specific task?
- Can you see links between, and then group together, related pieces of information?
- Can you form judgements about, and compare, information?
- Can you recognise the ways in which a writer creates a reaction in the reader?
- Can you use material from your reading to produce pieces of writing?

Don't panic! You have been building up your experience of these skills since you began reading.

How are these skills tested in examinations?

IGCSE First Language English tests your proficiency in these skills by setting a variety of question types, some of which ask you to use more than one skill at a time:

- short answer questions
- longer 'comprehension' questions (approximately one paragraph)
- summary tasks
- directed writing tasks.

It is very important that you recognise which skill or skills are being tested by each type of question, otherwise you may waste time giving the wrong type, or amount, of information in your answer.

Type of question	Skill 1	Skill 2	Skill 3	Skill 4
	Understand and explain meaning	Understand and explain implicit meaning	Select, collate, analyse, evaluate	Understand how writers achieve effects
Short answer [1 or 2 marks]	✓	✓	✓	
Longer answer		✓	✓	✓
Summary			✓	
Directed writing tasks	✓	✓	✓	

● **Try this** Copy the table below and see if you can decide which skill(s) each question is testing.

Question	Skill 1	Skill 2	Skill 3	Skill 4
1 Imagine that you are Bill and write his diary explaining what he likes and dislikes about his holiday.				
2 Write a summary of the attractions of Normandy in France for holidaymakers.				
3 What does 'recreation' mean?				
4 How does the writer make the beach seem an exciting place to be?				

TOPIC 2 Using reading skills: short answer questions

Key objectives

- To make sure that you understand what short answer questions are
- To help you to understand the way that short answer questions are marked by examiners
- To make sure that you understand the common mistakes that students make when tackling short answer questions
- To revise key strategies for approaching short answer questions

Key definitions

Term	Definition
Understand	To grasp the meaning of
Select	To pick out; to choose
Infer	To find out by a process of reasoning from something known
Deduce	To find out by a process of reasoning from a general rule or principle

Key ideas

Short answer questions are set only in Component 1 (Core); they:

- test understanding of specific words/phrases
- test understanding of specific ideas
- require you to select information that is relevant to the question.

More demanding short answer questions may:

- ask what you learn about a character in the text
- require you to infer attitudes/opinions from the text.

Common errors

Some students answer questions with answers that are plausible but not mentioned in the text. Wrong! ■

Some students give only one answer when a specific number have been requested. This means that not all marks available can be gained. ■

Sample questions and answers

Woody Norris may look like an insurance salesman but he's actually a genius inventor – and his latest gadget is set to revolutionise the way the world sounds

No one ever notices what's going on at a Radio Shack. Outside a lonely branch of the electronics store in a San Diego strip mall, where no one is noticing much of anything, a bluff man with thinning, ginger hair and preternaturally white teeth is standing on the pavement, slowly waving a square metal plate toward people strolling in the distance.

'Watch that lady over there,' he says, unable to conceal his boyish pride. 'This is really cool.' Woody Norris aims the silvery plate at his quarry. A brunette 200 feet away stops dead in her tracks and peers around, befuddled. She has walked straight into the noise of a Brazilian rainforest – then out again. 'Look at that,' Norris mutters, chuckling as the lady turns around. 'She doesn't know what hit her.'

Norris is demonstrating something called HyperSonic Sound (HSS) – the first revolution in acoustics since the

continued

loudspeaker was invented 78 years ago. The aluminum plate is connected to an amplifier that directs sound in a sharply demarcated column, much as a laser beam directs light. 'The way your brain perceives it, the sound is created right here,' Norris explains, lifting a palm to the side of his head. 'That's why it's so clear. Feels like it's inside your skull.' I pace out a hundred yards and see if the thing is really working. (HSS is so often suspected of being a parlour trick that it seems to bear checking.) Norris pelts me with Handel and, to illustrate the directionality of the beam, subtly turns the plate side to side. And the sound is inside my head, roving between my ears in accord with each of Norris's turns.

The applications of directional sound go way beyond messing with people at strip malls. Imagine, says Norris, walking by a soda machine (say, one of the five million in Japan that will soon employ HSS), triggering a proximity detector, then hearing what you alone hear – the plink of ice cubes and the invocation, 'Wouldn't a Coke taste great right about now?' Or riding in the family car, as the kids blast Eminem in the back seat while you and the wife play Tony Bennett up front. Or hearing targeted messages in every single aisle of a grocery store – for instance, near the fruit, 'Hey, it's the heart of kiwi season!' HyperSonic Sound has many other alluring features. An HSS transmission can travel 450 feet at practically the same volume all along its path. Translated: at a concert, there's no need to melt the eyebrows of people sitting in the front rows. And in past months Norris and the staff at his company, American Technology Corporation (ATC), have made a further, key improvement to HSS. Instead of sending out a column of sound, they can now project a single sphere of it, self-contained, like a bubble.

Sample question 1	State one effect of the HSS device shown in the first paragraph. [1 mark]
Student's answer	The HSS device upsets the lady.
Examiner's comments	*This answer is a little vague and does not gain a mark as the word* upsets *suggests distress whereas the passage describes the woman as* befuddled *which means confused.*
Sample question 2	How does Norris feel about his invention? [4 marks]
Student's answer	Norris is very obviously proud of his invention. He thinks that it is clever and innovative and he enjoys its effects.
Examiner's comments	*This is an excellent answer. The student has interpreted* boyish pride *and has offered an interpretation of* cool. *(S)he also offers* enjoys *to explain the final line of the paragraph. The two examples of interpretation alone would gain 4 marks.*
Sample question 3	Explain the meaning of the word 'pelts'. [1 mark]
Student's answer	A pelt is an animal skin.
Examiner's comments	*This answer is incorrect. Although in another context a pelt is an animal skin it is clearly not the meaning being used in this passage. Using deduction it should be clear that the word which is missing is a verb not a noun.*
Sample question 4	Explain the meaning of the phrase 'messing with people'. [2 marks]
Student's answer	Messing with people seems to mean confusing or creating a muddle. Usually if something is in a mess it is untidy. The man has been confusing people with his invention.
Examiner's comments	*This answer gains 2 marks as the student has offered a plausible interpretation and a reason for it.*

Sample question 5 Give three advantages of directional sound from paragraph 3. [3 marks]

Student's answer Directional sound is useful because it can mean that only one person hears something at a time, or that different people in a small space can listen to different things, and also that lots of people can hear something at the same volume, even if they are further away.

Examiner's comments *This is a good answer. Although the advantages are not concisely or clearly expressed the student has understood three distinct features of HSS, so gains 3 marks.*

Examiner's tips
▶ Remember that *everything* you write should be based on *what you have read in the passage.*
▶ You should *not* use your imagination to think of reactions to the sounds.
▶ You should *not* add information about HSS, even if you have heard of it before.
▶ If you are not familiar with a word, try to work it out from the words around it and by using your powers of deduction.

● **Try this**
- Read the passage *Life on Inishmaan* below, taken from a past exam paper.
- Read the following short answer questions set on it.
- Then look at the students' answers that have been provided.
- Look at the answer guide on **pages 7–8**, which the examiner used to mark these responses. What marks would you give? (Answers are given on **page 91**.)

● Life on Inishmaan

This passage is part of an account written 100 years ago by a man who went to live on Inishmaan, a remote island off the west coast of Ireland. It describes his first journey to his new home, and his impressions of it.

Early this morning the man of the house came over for me with a *curagh* – that is, a boat with four rowers and four oars on either side, as each man uses two — and we set off a little before noon.

It gave me a moment of exquisite satisfaction to find myself moving away from civilisation in this rough canvas canoe of a type that has served primitive races since people first went on the sea.

We had to stop for a moment at a vessel that is anchored in the bay, to make some arrangements for the fish-processing. When we started again, a small sail was run up in the bow, and we set off across the water with a leaping up-and-down motion that had no resemblance to the heavy movement of a larger boat. The sail is used only as an aid, so the men continued to row after it had gone up, and as they occupied the four cross-seats, I lay on the canvas at the stern and on the frame of slender wooden laths, which bent and quivered as the waves passed under them.

When we set off it was a brilliant morning of April, and the green, glittering waves seemed to toss the canoe among themselves, yet as we drew nearer this island a sudden thunderstorm broke out behind the rocks we were approaching, and caused a momentary tumult in this still vein of the Atlantic.

5 ●

We landed at a small pier, from which a rough track leads up to the village between small fields and bare sheets of rock like those in Aranmor. The youngest son of my boatman, a boy of about seventeen, who is to be my teacher and guide, was waiting for me at the pier and guided me to his house, while the men settled the *curagh* and followed slowly with my baggage.

My room is at one end of the cottage, with a boarded floor and ceiling, and two windows opposite each other. Then there is the kitchen with earth floor and open rafters, and two doors opposite each other opening into the open air, but no windows. Beyond it there are two small rooms of half the width of the kitchen with one window apiece.

The kitchen itself, where I will spend most of my time, is full of beauty and distinction. The red dresses of the women who cluster round the fire on their stools give a glow of almost Eastern richness, and the walls have been toned by the turf smoke to a soft brown that blends with the grey earth-colour of the floor. Many sorts of fishing-tackle, the nets, and the oiled skins worn by the fishermen are hung upon the walls or among the open rafters; and right overhead, under the thatch, there is a whole skin from which they make leather sandals.

Every article on these islands has an almost personal character, which gives this simple life, where all art is unknown, a natural artistic beauty. The *curaghs* and spinning-wheels, the tiny wooden barrels that are still much used in place of earthenware, the home-made cradles, churns, and baskets, are all full of individuality; being made from materials that are common here, they seem to exist as a natural link between the people and the world about them.

1 What is a *curagh*? Explain what it is made of.   [4 marks]

2 Quote **three** words from the passage that describe the thunderstorm or the effect it had upon the sea.   [3 marks]

3 Give **three** things in the kitchen that especially caught the writer's attention.   [3 marks]

4 With close reference to the passage, explain what you think the writer liked best about:
   i) the voyage to the island
   ii) the articles he found on the island.   [4 marks]

Student A's answers

1 It is a fishing boat with 4 rowers and 4 oars on either side and it is made of wood and traditional things.

2 i) Cause momentary tumult.
   ii) Sound which is effective.
   iii) Killing of people around that place.

3 i) Whole skin from which they make leather sandals.
   ii) The red dresses of the women who cluster round the fire on their stools, give a glow of almost Eastern richness.
   iii) The walls have have been toned by the turf smoke to a soft brown that blends with the grey earth-colour of the floor.

4 i) The voyage to the island:
  - He liked the boat which was made by traditional things.
  - He was quite happy to find himself moving from civilisation in that rough canvas canoe of a type that has served primitive races since people first went on the sea.

ii) The articles he found on the island:
  - They were made from that island (home-made) by people themself from that island.
  - They were so attractive to his/her eyes when he saw them.

Student B's answers 1 The curagh was made of wood from the forest and four rowers and a sail with laths and four cross seats.

2 i) Sudden.
   ii) Broke.
   iii) Vein.

3 i) Beauty.
   ii) Distinction.
   iii) The red dresses.

4 i) What the writer liked about the voyage is that he was leaving from civilisation and he is going to see other places with interesting articles and Nature.
   ii) What the writer liked about the articles he found on the island was different from what he tought it will be. he was amaze by the life on that island like the house where he stayed it had no windows opposite each other and in the kitchen there was beautiful design of women in red dresses.

Answer guide 1 What is a *curagh*? Explain what it is made of. [4 marks]

  - a boat/canoe
  - propelled with oars/has rowers/oarsmen
  - of traditional design
  - with a sail
  - made of canvas
  - made of wood
  - (boat) with an unusual motion

Give 1 mark for reference to any of these points, up to a maximum of 4.

2 Give three words from the passage that describe the thunderstorm or the effect it had upon the sea. [3 marks]

  - sudden
  - momentary
  - tumult

Give 1 mark for each point. If 'momentary tumult' is given as one answer, award both marks.

3 Give three things about the kitchen that especially caught the writer's attention. [3 marks]

- red/coloured (dresses of the women)
- colour of the walls
- colour of the floor
- fishing tackle on walls
- the skin (for making sandals)

Give 1 mark for each point up to a maximum of 3.

4 With close reference to the passage, explain what you think the writer liked best about:
   i) the voyage to the island
   ii) the articles he found on the island. [4 marks]

- *Either* he was leaving civilised life behind and travelling in a boat whose design had never changed/of traditional design/the fine weather/thunderstorm/green glittering waves

   Or any reference to the unusual motion of the boat (leaping through waves etc.)

- Handmade out of natural materials, thus having individual, unique quality and/or an art of their own.

Give up to 2 marks per section. For each, 1 mark for a recognisable answer and 2 for a fuller answer with an attempt to explain. Give 0 for injudicious copying.

How to improve your answers

1 Read the questions carefully

It is very important that you read the question *slowly* and *carefully* and work out what kind of question you are answering before you start writing.

Whilst you read, get into the habit of copying the question and underlining, highlighting or annotating the key words. The following are example questions to show how you could do this:

a) <u>What was</u> John's main method of transport in the town? *This is a question that tests understanding of specific ideas.*

b) What is <u>meant by</u> 'vintage vehicle'? *This is a question that tests understanding of specific words/phrases.*

c) What do you <u>learn about John</u> in paragraph 3? *This is a question that asks what you learn about a character in the text.*

d) What are <u>John's parents' views</u> about his hobby? Use paragraph 3 only. *This is a question that requires you to deduce or interpret attitudes/opinions from the text.*

● **Try this**   Look at the following example questions. What are the key words in each? What kind of question is each one?

1 Find three reasons why Elsa is happy to go to school.
2 What is a peninsula?
3 Name two features of the landscape in Brittany.
4 What is the teacher like in paragraph 4?

2 Do only what the question asks you to

- Be careful to read the question carefully so that you know exactly what you are looking for.
- Take care that you read the correct part of the passage. Sometimes there may be information that seems to be relevant elsewhere in the passage. If you read it, or include it in your answer, you will waste time.
- Make sure you know how many points to make. The question may tell you or the number of marks may give you a clue.

● **Try this** Look back at the answer guide on **pages 7–8**. Study the number of marks allocated to each question and the way that the answer guide awarded them.

3 Unsure about a word?

Don't panic if you are unsure about the meaning of a word. You need only grasp the gist of most of the passage.

However, if the word you are confused by is in a question, or seems to be necessary to work out an answer, then try to work it out. Look at what type of word it is (noun, verb, adjective or adverb). Next work out what meaning would complete the sentence fluently.

● **Try this** Read the following sentences and, using deduction, work out the meaning of the words in italics.

1 He had done this last year in the junior class and it had been easy for him then. How could this possibly be a test for him now? James completed the *facile* task rapidly without even breaking into a sweat.

2 The small submarine gave us a perfect view of the sea bed. A *gribble* was boring a hole in the piece of wood on the sea floor, its seven pairs of legs waving excitedly in the current. Other creatures passed by warily. We were only interested in finding the wreck.

3 It was a beautiful night. The sky was clear and inky black. There were no buildings or street lights to light our way but we had no problem. The *lucent* stars were silver in the night sky, allowing us to see the moon clearly.

4 Use your own words

As far as possible use your own words in answers, particularly when explaining the meaning of words or phrases.

5 Include all relevant details

In your answer be sure to include all details that are relevant. Do not miss out any point just because it seems obvious.

> **Key revision points**
> - Understand that short answer questions are a test of reading only.
> - Read and analyse the question before reading the passage.
> - Highlight or underline possible answers as you read the passage.
> - When reading, use deduction to work out the meaning of any key words but don't worry if you don't understand every word.
> - When writing your answer, use your own words as far as possible.
> - When writing your answer, include even obvious details.

TOPIC 3 Using reading skills: understand how writers achieve effects

Key objectives

- To make sure that you understand what writers' effects are
- To help you to understand the way that questions about writers' effects are marked by examiners
- To make sure that you understand the common mistakes that students make when tackling this type of question
- To revise key strategies for approaching writers' effects questions

Key definition

Term	Definition
Writer's effect	The effect on the reader created by an author's words. This effect could be to stimulate our sense of sight, touch, hearing or even smell. It could be to convey a scene, idea or emotion

Key ideas

After reading a passage you need to work out *what* effect the writer has created. Here is a checklist of possibilities:

- An experience has been described.
- An atmosphere has been created.
- A statement of fact has been made.
- An opinion/emotion has been conveyed.
- A reaction has been provoked.

Next you need to work out what *impression* has been made on your mind or senses. Here is a checklist of possibilities:

- You can see the scene that has been described.
- You can hear the sounds that have been described.
- You can almost smell or taste something that was described.
- You can almost physically or emotionally feel something described.

Finally you need to understand *what caused* this effect on you. Here is a checklist of possible causes:

- The specific meaning of a word.
- The associations created by a word.
- The rhythm and pace of words and sentence structures.
- The positioning of words, phrases, sentences and lines on the page.

Common misconceptions

Some students think that understanding a writer's effect means just saying whether or not you like a piece of writing. This is only a small part of how a writer affects you. ■

Some students think that understanding a writer's effect means quoting some words which have an effect on you and copying them out. Using quotations is only one part of the process; explaining how and why it affects you is the main part. ■

Sample questions and answers

Sample question 1 This is in a simple format.

Re-read the following lines from the main passage. Pick out three words or phrases that the writer uses to show that the man was distressed about the damage done to his car. How do they reveal his feelings?

> 'I cannot believe it!' James bellowed, his face red with rage. Sweat beaded his forehead as he stared in disbelief at the scratch marks which ran along the full length of his beautiful Rolls Royce. 'My beautiful, beautiful baby … ruined.' His voice trailed off in despair.

Student's answer I can tell the man is angry when the writer uses the words 'bellowed', 'red with rage' and 'trailed off in despair'. 'Bellowed' is a very powerful word meaning a loud cry, which would suggest he is very angry. Red is a colour which I associate with danger. People go red when they are furious. Finally when he trails off I imagine someone so upset they cannot speak anymore.

Examiner's comments *This is a fairly good answer. The answer is clearly focused on the task. The candidate picks out one single word and two phrases which show anger. The candidate attempts to explain how the examples create an impression of anger by referring to the precise meanings of the words, simple associations that (s)he has made with the words and how they create an impression of the emotion in her/his mind. The final example would have been more effective if punctuation had been referred to.*

Sample question 2 This is more complex.

By referring closely to the language used by the writer in the following lines from the main passage, explain how she communicates:
a) the violence of the girl's actions
b) ~~her~~ feelings about the girl's behaviour. ⤴ his (typo)

> 'I hate you!' the girl screamed like a banshee, her voice grating and harsh. 'I'm never coming back, never!' Her words were accompanied by a horrifying crash as the glass panes in the window shattered one by one until they lay in a jagged heap, just like his shattered dreams.

Student's answer   a) The girl's behaviour is clearly violent. The word 'screamed' is very strong, suggesting high volume and a lack of control. The simile 'like a banshee' suggests that she is almost supernatural. Saying that the glass breaking makes a 'horrifying' noise clearly suggests it is loud enough to make someone feel very shocked.

Examiner's comments   *This is a good answer which refers to several examples and explains them fully.*

Student's answer   b) 'Like a banshee' makes me think that the writer sees her as quite frightening, as a banshee would be. She also describes the girl's voice as 'grating' which suggests it is unpleasant to the writer, almost having an abrasive effect. The breaking of the glass is very unnecessary and is usually seen as anti-social which makes me feel that the writer is intentionally giving us a negative impression of the girl, and anyway, the writer seems to sympathise more with the man because she describes his 'shattered dreams' and invokes pity for him, not the girl.

Examiner's comments   *This is an excellent answer as the candidate explains in some detail exactly how the writer's attitude is shown, referring to precise meanings of words, associations which the words used by the writer evoke and the way in which the writer's viewpoint manipulates the reader's sympathy.*

Examiner's tips
The examiner has helped you by writing the questions in such a way that:
▶ You are told what some of the impressions produced on the mind or senses are – distress (Question 1), violence (Question 2).
   However, Question 2b) *does not* tell you exactly what to look for. It gives you only a clue that a feeling is shown. You have to work out which feeling. This is helpful because you know that you are not looking for an idea or opinion. (This answer would be worth more marks than an answer where you were told what to look for.)
▶ You are told where to look for the cause of the impressions – three words or phrases (Question 1), the language used by the writer (Question 2).

● **Try this**   • Read the passage below.
   • Read the writer's effect question set on it.
   • Then look at the students' answers that have been provided.
   • Look at the answer guide on **page 13**, which the examiner used to mark these responses. What marks would you give? (Answers are given on **page 91**.)

'There,' he said to the class. 'Your teacher has a snake around her neck and she's not afraid.'
   Miss Aitcheson stood rigid; she seemed to be holding her breath.
   'Teacher's not afraid, are you?' the attendant persisted. He leaned forward, pronouncing judgement on her, while she suddenly jerked her head and lifted her hands in panic to get rid of the snake. Then, seeing the children watching her, she whispered, 'No, I'm not afraid. Of course not.' She looked around her.
   'Of course not,' she repeated sharply.
   I could see her defeat and helplessness. The attendant seemed unaware, as if his perception had grown a reptilian covering.

'See, Miss Aitcheson's touching the snake. She's not afraid of it at all.'
As everyone watched, she touched the snake. Her fingers recoiled.
She touched it again.

'See, she's not afraid. Miss Aitcheson can stand there with a beautiful snake around her neck and touch it and stroke it and not be afraid.'

How does the writer convey Miss Aitcheson's fear in this passage?[10 marks]

Student C's answer I can tell that the teacher is very frightened because it says that she stands 'rigid'. It also says that she is holding her breath. Later on she jerks her head and lifts her hands up to get rid of the snake.

Student D's answer The teacher's fear is shown by the way she acts and speaks. The writer really helps us to see that she is so frightened she can hardly move. She is probably scared that if she does, the snake will strike. He uses words like 'rigid' which suggests she is almost stiff like a statue and 'jerked' which again suggests that she is not at all relaxed. I can almost feel the teacher's fear because the passage says that she is holding her breath. I know that this makes me feel panicky and very still and stiff. This is a very effective way of showing me how she feels.

Answer guide

Band	Marks	Criteria
1	9–10	Wide ranging discussion of language with high quality comments that add meanings and associations to words and demonstrate the writer's reasons for using them. May group choices of words to identify writer's objectives
2	7–8	Reference is made to a good number of words and phrases, some of which identify the intended effects. There is evidence that the student understands the intention of the exercise
3	5–6	A satisfactory attempt to identify appropriate words and phrases. The answer gives meanings of words but does not identify effects
4	3–4	Student selects words although weaker words may be included while stronger words are neglected. Explanations are noticeably less well done and do not add much to the choice of words
5	1–2	The choice of words is insecure. While the question has been understood, there is no evidence that the writer's choice of language has been appreciated
6	0	Answers do not fit the question. Inappropriate words and phrases are chosen

How to improve your answers

1 Read the question carefully

The examiner will give you all of your directions in the question. It is very important that you read it *slowly* and *carefully* so that you don't miss anything.

Remember that you are looking for three things:

- Does the question tell you what effect you are looking for?
- Does the question tell you where to look for the effect?
- Does the question tell you how the effect is created?

13 ●

Whilst you read, get into the habit of noting down the directions. For example:

*Where to look   What effect you
for the effect   are looking for*

Read lines 33–38. What opinion does the writer have of the big game hunters? How do the comparisons he chooses tell you this?

*How the effect
is created*

● **Try this** Copy the example questions below and underline, highlight or annotate each one to clarify exactly what you are being asked to do.

1 Pick out two phrases that express the strength of the wind. How do they emphasise its power?

2 How does the writer create a tense atmosphere at the start of the story?

3 How do the words chosen by the author make the description of Mr Hibbins amusing?

2 Be as precise as possible when identifying effects

Being precise shows the examiner that you have carefully considered the words of the passage and have reached a conclusion about their effect. You may need to build your vocabulary so that you can make specific statements.

● **Try this** 1 Writers often create an atmosphere. Look up the following words in a dictionary. They could all be used to describe a negative atmosphere between two people, but they also imply subtle variations in emotion.

- Tense
- Hostile
- Unpleasant
- Aggressive
- Volatile

Which is the most negative word, of the five above, to apply to a relationship? Which is the least?

2 Writers often want us to understand a character's emotions. List six words that could be used to describe an emotion felt by someone who is feeling positive about a situation. One has been done for you.

- Happy

3 In a media piece a writer often has an opinion or attitude towards the topic (s)he is discussing. Here are some words and phrases to describe this. Copy these out and explain the attitude of the writer for each.

- Supportive
- In accord with
- Dubious about
- Opposed to
- Broadly in favour of
- Horrified by
- Cautiously optimistic about
- Distressed by

3 Quote selectively from the passage

You will only ever be quoting single words or brief phrases. If you are copying out more than this then you are not showing that you can accurately judge exactly how an effect is being created. You are simply showing where the effect might be.

Compare the following two incomplete answers.

Student's answer   I felt tense when I read: 'The car teetered on the edge of the cliff with its wheels dangling over the edge. The horn continued to sound as the gulls shrieked around the bonnet.'

Examiner's comments   *This is a poor answer. It shows us broadly where in the passage the feeling of tension was created but does not identify a key word or phrase and does not explain specifically how the tension was created.*

Student's answer   I felt tense when I read that the car 'teetered on the edge' because the word teetered suggests that it was rocking unsteadily, meaning that it could tip over at any minute. I can see it hanging there on the cliff and I feel tense waiting to see what will happen.

Examiner's comments   *This is an excellent answer. It identifies a key word which creates tension and then explains how it does so by referring to the explicit meaning of the word and the visual image it creates. The answer then explains how these lead to a reaction in the reader.*

● **Try this**   Read this description of a neglected house. It creates a distinctly ominous atmosphere. Write down the key words or phrases that particularly contribute to this atmosphere. (You should not pick out more than three words at a time.)

The drive was a ribbon now, a thread of its former self, with gravel surface gone, and choked with grass and moss. The trees had thrown out low branches, making an impediment to progress; the gnarled roots looked like skeleton claws. Scattered here and again amongst this jungle growth I would recognize shrubs that had been landmarks in our time, things of culture and grace, hydrangeas whose blue heads had been famous. No hand had checked their progress, and they had gone native now, rearing to monster height without a bloom, black and ugly as the nameless parasites that grew beside them.

On and on, now east now west, wound the poor thread that once had been our drive. Sometimes I thought it lost, but it appeared again, beneath a fallen tree perhaps, or struggling on the other side of a muddied ditch created by the winter rains. I had not thought the way so long. Surely the miles had multiplied, even as the trees had done, and this path led but to a labyrinth, some choked wilderness, and not to the house at all. I came upon it suddenly; the

approach masked by the unnatural growth of a vast shrub that spread in all directions, and I stood, my heart thumping in my breast, the strange prick of tears behind my eyes.

There was Manderley, our Manderley, secretive and silent as it had always been, the grey stone shining in the moonlight of my dream, the mullioned windows reflecting the green lawns and the terrace. Time could not wreck the perfect symmetry of those walls, nor the site itself, a jewel in the hollow of a hand.

The terrace sloped to the lawns, and the lawns stretched to the sea, and turning I could see the sheet of silver placid under the moon, like a lake undisturbed by wind or storm. No waves would come to ruffle this dream water, and no bulk of cloud, wind-driven from the west, obscure the clarity of this pale sky. I turned again to the house, and though it stood inviolate, untouched, as though we ourselves had left but yesterday, I saw that the garden had obeyed the jungle law, even as the woods had done. The rhododendrons stood fifty feet high, twisted and entwined with bracken, and they had

---

continued

entered into alien marriage with a host of nameless shrubs, poor, bastard things that clung about their roots as though conscious of their spurious origin. A lilac had mated with a copper beech, and to bind them yet more closely to one another the malevolent ivy, always an enemy to grace, had thrown her tendrils about the pair and made them prisoners. Ivy held prior place in this lost garden, the long strands crept across the lawns, and soon would encroach upon the house itself. There was another plant too, some half-breed from the woods, whose seed had been scattered long ago beneath the trees and then forgotten, and now, marching in unison with the ivy, thrust its ugly form like a giant rhubarb towards the soft grass where the daffodils had blown.

Nettles were everywhere, the vanguard of the army. They choked the terrace, they sprawled about the paths, they leant, vulgar and lanky, against the very windows of the house. They made indifferent sentinels, for in many places their ranks had been broken by the rhubarb plant, and they lay with crumpled heads and listless stems, making a pathway for the rabbits. I left the drive and went to the terrace, for the nettles were no barrier to me, a dreamer. I walked enchanted, and nothing held me back.

4 Explain how the writer creates the effect

Once you have identified the effect that has been produced and where proof of it can be found, you must next explain *how the proof shows the effect* that you have claimed is there. At IGCSE level there are three major types of proof expected.

a) Use the precise meaning of a word to explain how it creates the effect

There are many words in the English language that mean roughly the same thing. Writers choose words carefully to create a specific meaning. This in turn will often create a specific effect.

For example, imagine that a writer is describing a character who is very aggressive. This source passage contains a description of the character unpacking some shopping:

> Hiteshi slammed the packets down on the counter. Her fingers gripped the cardboard carton so hard that her finger-nails left crescent shaped indentations in the egg box. Thrusting her hand into the carrier bag she pinched the corner of a packet and wrenched it towards her with fury.

Look at the verbs chosen by the writer to describe the unpacking process:

gripped   *thrusting*   *pinched*   *wrenched*

The dictionary tells us that these words all involve force, the possibility of pain and intensity. These definitions could be used to support our impression that the character is aggressive.

Sample answer Hiteshi is an aggressive woman. She cannot perform a simple domestic task without behaving in an over-forceful, possibly damaging way. When the writer tells us that she 'gripped' and 'pinched' the shopping it is as if she were holding on to it very tightly, far more tightly than is necessary, as if she wanted to hurt it.

● **Try this** Write a paragraph focusing on the verbs used to describe the way Hiteshi moves her hands.

b) Use the 'strength' of a word to explain how it creates the effect

There are many words in the English language that mean roughly the same thing. Writers choose words carefully to create a specific intensity or strength of meaning. This in turn will often create a very specific effect.

For example, imagine that a writer is describing one character who hates another. The source passage contains a description of the character confronting her enemy:

> Kiera took a deep breath and walked towards Vicki. Feelings of disgust grew inside her and she knew there was no turning back. 'Do you know just how much I despise you?' she spat. 'You repulse me, you revolt me. I hate you!' Suddenly she could bear no more. Gritting her teeth she turned and marched away; head held high.

Look at the words chosen by the writer to describe Kiera's dislike for Vicki:

disgust   *despise*   *repulse*   *revolt*

● **Try this**   There are many other words that could be used to express dislike, such as:

dislike	animosity	repugnance	horror
abhor	pique	loathing	detest
disfavour	grudge	abomination	nauseate
odium	acrimony	antipathy	antagonise

1 Draw a scale like this.

   Weak dislike   Strong dislike

   Try to place as many of the above words as you can on the scale.
2 Where would the four words used by the writer to describe Kiera's dislike of Vicki be placed?
3 What does this tell you about the strength and specific nature of Kiera's feelings?
4 Write a paragraph summing up your findings.

c) Use the associations of a word to explain how it creates the effect

There are many words in the English language that mean roughly the same thing. Writers choose words carefully to create a specific set of ideas in our minds. The set of ideas in our minds in turn will often create a very specific effect.

These ideas may:

- be a set of visual images; for instance, if someone is described as a sloth we envisage someone who is sleepy and slow moving, and so we think that the person described is lazy
- consist of other sensory impressions; for instance, if someone is described as a mouse we imagine a very quiet person, which may lead us to think that the person is shy or timid

- consist of distinctive atmospheres/emotions; for instance, if someone describes a party as funereal some people would understand this to mean sombre and unamusing, which leads us to consider that the party described was not enjoyable.

● **Try this**   1   Copy the following two lists then match up the words chosen with the set of ideas they create. One has been done for you.

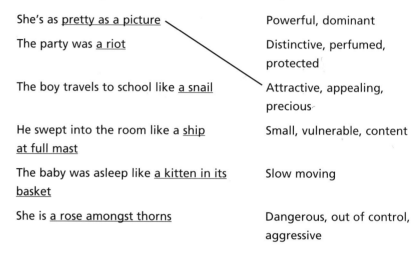

She's as <u>pretty as a picture</u>

The party was <u>a riot</u>

The boy travels to school like <u>a snail</u>

He swept into the room like a <u>ship at full mast</u>

The baby was asleep like <u>a kitten in its basket</u>

She is <u>a rose amongst thorns</u>

Powerful, dominant

Distinctive, perfumed, protected

Attractive, appealing, precious

Small, vulnerable, content

Slow moving

Dangerous, out of control, aggressive

2   Now write a paragraph describing the ideas created in your mind by any one of the phrases above.

5 Look out for more than one effect

Be aware that there may be more than one effect in the same piece of writing. A good writer is always trying to do as much as possible in as few words as possible, and so will choose words and phrases that do lots of things at the same time. One word may:

- create a very specific meaning
- create a very specific level of intensity or strength
- create a visual picture
- stimulate your senses
- create an atmosphere
- stimulate emotions.

For example, imagine that a writer is describing a character. The following line describes a character entering a room:

> Xavier burst through the door, a rhinoceros of a man.

When we read this our mind is immediately full of a variety of ideas produced by the word rhinoceros:

Sample answer The writer creates a number of impressions about Xavier by using the word 'rhinoceros' to describe him. First, I get a visual image of a large, solidly built man. I imagine his skin to be weathered and thickened by sun and wind. He may have grey hair or a greying complexion. I also get the idea that Xavier is quite formidable. He may be aggressive and fearless. He could be quite a tense person, always alone and alert. From all of this I feel that I should be wary of him.

● **Try this** Write down the different impressions you have when you see someone described as 'a pussycat'.

● **Try this** Read this persuasive letter which was sent out by a charity called The Camphill Family which provides homes for people unable to live independently. It portrays the community as a very positive and caring place to be.

Pick out the words or phrases which particularly contribute to the creation of this attitude.

Dear Friend

Nicky works in a café, is an opera fan and a mean draughts player. If you were to see him at work, I think you'd be struck by his evident pride in his job and the elegant bow tie he wears. I'm sure you'd also notice that he has Down's Syndrome.

Here in a Camphill community, Nicky and many other people in need of special care and understanding have a chance to make the most of every minute of their lives. They have the support to work, learn and contribute to their community in a way that might simply not be possible elsewhere.

Nicky, like me, lives in The Croft Community in Malton, North Yorkshire. It is one of eleven communities in Britain supported by The Camphill Family, and registered as a charity called the Camphill Village Trust. 'It's great, living here', he says. 'Working in the café where I meet the public has made me more confident with people.'

Every Camphill community has a unique character. There are communities for those who enjoy living in a town, like The Croft, as well as places set amidst the beauty and tranquillity of the countryside. Home can be with others or in one's own house or flat with the support of caring friends nearby. Nicky chooses to live in an extended family home with me, my wife and children, and six other good friends.

Wherever we live, work is a fundamental part of our lives. Everyone does the jobs that best suit their abilities and personality. Nicky, for example, has two very different jobs. Along with working in our café in Malton town centre, he is a fantastic help in our community garden. As he puts it: 'We grow our own vegetables from seed and there are always jobs to do.'

Like all our sister Camphill communities, The Croft has a variety of craft workshops. Together, we make beautiful items which we successfully market in Britain and abroad – on their own merits, not as having been made by people with special needs. Those of us who live in rural locations also farm and produce food of the highest organic quality.

The first Camphill community was founded in Scotland over sixty years ago, by a pioneering doctor called Karl König. He believed that everyone has talents – no matter how disabled they might appear – and should have the

continued

chance to develop their potential in an atmosphere of mutual care and respect. Since then, Camphill communities have been living, breathing, practical examples of how this ideal can be achieved. Today over 500 adults with special needs in Britain have a home with us.

I appreciate you taking the time to read my letter. I do hope you will decide that you can help Nicky and his friends, and in advance, I'd like to thank you so much for your kindness.

With warmest regards

John Carlile

John Carlile,
Houseparent, The Croft Community

Key revision points

- Understand that questions on reading skills are a test of *reading* only.
- Read and analyse the question before reading the passage.
- When writing your answer, always quote examples from the passage.
- When writing your answer, always explain how the effects have been created by specific details and features in the passage.

TOPIC 4 Using reading skills: directed writing task

Key objectives

- To make sure that you understand what directed writing is
- To help you to understand the way that directed writing is marked by examiners
- To make sure that you understand the common mistakes that students make when tackling directed writing tasks
- To revise key strategies for approaching directed writing tasks

Key definition

Term	Definition
Directed writing	'To direct' means to have authority or control over or to instruct to do something. Directed writing is where you are told exactly how to write and about what

Key ideas

Directed writing is set in Component 3 (Core and Extended). It is where the examiner is *directing* you about:

- who to write as
- who to write for
- how to write
- what to write about – all ideas and information should come from the source text.

Common misconceptions

Some students think that directed writing is based on ideas from their imagination. This is a dangerous misconception and can lead to a very low mark being awarded. ▪

Some students think that their actual writing – paragraphing, spelling and grammar – does not matter in directed writing. This is not always true. If in doubt, check the answer guide. ▪

Sample question and answers

Sample question Read the passage about Riga on the next page. Imagine that your parents take you there for a holiday. Using standard English, write an e-mail to a friend at home, describing what you have been doing and how you feel about your holiday destination.

Riga is a fairytale city. The Latvian capital has cobbled squares, idiosyncratic museums, heavenly coffee shops and buskers on every street corner. Despite a troubled history – Latvia only shook off communism in 1991 – Riga's historic buildings are amazingly well preserved. The heart of the city is largely medieval, with tiny streets wiggling past churches and grand guildhalls. It feels like a Toytown film set, partly because there are no cars and partly due to its 'wealth of legends'. The bell of St Jacob's church, for instance, was once rumoured to ring every time an unfaithful wife passed beneath the spire.

The city also boasts some of the finest Art Nouveau buildings in Europe. Built at the turn of the last century, when Riga was the largest trading port in the Russian empire, they constitute a riot of

architectural fantasies. Alberta Street is the best example: the buildings are adorned with sphinxes, roaring lions and rooftop arches. In the afternoons, the park is the place to be. Even when it's chilly, people come here to snooze, read papers, listen to the buskers (Latvians are mad about every kind of music) and play chess. It's like 'slipping between the pages of *Gorky Park*'.

If you fancy some culture, you'll be spoilt for choice. There are museums and galleries galore. The Porcelain Museum is 'tiny and exquisite'; the Photography Museum has 'spine-tingling' photographs taken with the world's first spy camera; the Museum of the Occupation of Latvia makes grim but fascinating viewing. In the evening, visit the Latvian Opera House where a front-row ticket costs around £4. ★

Examiner's tips

▶ The examiner has given you a lot of *directions* in this question:
  ▶ who to write as – *yourself*
  ▶ who to write for – *a friend*
  ▶ how to write – *in standard English as if in an e-mail, that is, like a letter*
  ▶ what to write about – *what you have been doing (in Riga) and how you feel about Riga.*
▶ Remember that *everything* you write should be based on what you have read in the passage.
▶ You *should*:
  ▶ write about what the passage tells you, as if you were there
  ▶ choose to write as if you either liked or disliked the city, based on what you have read about its attractions.
▶ You *should not*:
  ▶ use your imagination to think of extra activities
  ▶ add information about Riga, even if you have been there.

Student's answer

Hi, Suzanna. Just a quick e-mail to let you know that we are here. (Yawn) I can't believe that Mum and Dad have brought me half way around the world just to look at architecture and visit museums full of cups and saucers! They spend the whole time going on about how amazing it is to see so many historic buildings that haven't been knocked down or spoilt. I find it a bit boring – although there are some weird statues and things. We saw one house with a stone lion on its roof!

I suppose there are some good points – lots of music to listen to as we wander around. (My feet ache!) I gave some money to a guy who was playing a really good version of your favourite Oasis track. There are some really good coffee shops for cake! Oh and there are no cars – they don't allow them for some reason. To be fair there is also a good park. I had a game of chess with some kid while Mum read the paper and Dad had a nap.

The guidebook says that this used to be the biggest trading port in the Russian Empire which is why everything is so decorated and well maintained. There are quite a few stories about the city and what happened here … but they're not exactly Harry Potter!

Well, must go. We're off to the Opera tonight. Mum says it'll be worth it just to see the theatre which is supposed to be very pretty.

Tomorrow they've got a whole day of looking at photographs planned. I can't wait to get home to satellite TV! Bye!

Examiner's comments *This is a good response. The student has clearly read and understood the passage. (S)he refers to many of the attractions on offer in Riga and adds some detail and comments without straying too far from the passage. The material is well ordered, combining related attractions and examples. (S)he also creates a convincing 'voice' and writes accurately and clearly in standard English.*

Student's answer Yo, Deepak! Riga is awesome! I have been to nightclubs every night and have slept most of the day. The olds are totally in love with all the old buildings and history. Sad or what? Thank goodness I found Macdonalds as some of the food is a bit odd.

I managed to get on to level 4 on *Mizzadventure* – have you got there yet? I spent the whole plane journey on it. There are some good cheats on that site you told me about.

Mum and Dad are never in. See you soon mate. Can't wait to get home to my Playstation.

Examiner's comments *This is a poor response. The student has not used much of the material from the passage. The only explicit reference is to the 'old buildings'. Instead most of the information in the e-mail is about activities that (s)he has made up. This means that it is impossible to assess whether or not (s)he read and understood the passage.*

Although the e-mail is clearly in the 'voice' of a teenager, the examination question stated that standard English should be used. This response uses slang. In addition the response has no real sense of order, with comments randomly organised.

● **Try this**
- Read the programme and diary extract below, taken from a past exam paper.
- Read the directed writing question set on it.
- Then look at the students' answers that have been provided.
- Note down anything in their answers that is clearly based on the passage.
- Look at the answer guide on **page 26,** which the examiner used to mark these responses. What marks would you give? (Answers are given on **page 91**.)

● Programme

Day 1 Arrival and acclimatisation	**Day 4** Rest day with team games
Day 2 Rock climbing and visit to waterfall	**Day 5** Shooting the rapids
Day 3 Jungle trek	**Day 6** Return

Patchara's diary

Day 1

Terrible journey. The truck jolted and bumped and we were thrown up and down till we ached. All right for Miss Ishida and Mr Enberg – they were up front with the driver. Miss Ishida said it would help to toughen us up. Oh! and the weather – it's so humid, I feel like lying on the ground and staying there. Our living quarters are unspeakable. We're all close together, the beds are hard, and someone has smelly feet, ugh! Mr Enberg says it teaches us to live together and reminds us what real life is like. Where's the aircon?

Day 2

I hate this. I was humiliated. I never wanted to go up the rock face, but they made me. Everything was steaming and the rock was covered with vegetation so it wasn't exactly dangerous, but I panicked. Two-thirds up I was sure I was going to fall, so I froze. I was the tenth to go so there they were at the top and the bottom, staring at me spreadeagled. But no one laughed. Mr Enberg was just behind me and he helped me to the top. I didn't know teachers could be so kind. And when I got there they all clapped. In the afternoon they took us to a marvellous waterfall – I don't think I've ever seen anything so beautiful, and Miss Ishida says we must fight to prevent countryside like that from being destroyed. I was gawping at the top when I fell in, just like that, and had to be rescued for the second time that day. I thought I'd drown. This time they did laugh, but in the end I joined in.

Day 3

They made us dress up so that the leeches couldn't get us. Sunida didn't do it and got them all over her. We had to look after her. I guess it was her bad day. You sort of get used to living uncomfortably – and everything you do is public. So you have to rely on your friends. When I saw the snake gliding towards me, they were there to warn me not to panic. And I wasn't really afraid, not as I thought I would be. But it was great seeing the monkeys and the parrots. And Mr Enberg showed me a fungus he said contained a drug to fight cancer. I got back dripping and looking like a rubbish heap, but I'd had a great day. Afterwards they told us that that part of the jungle was in danger of being felled.

Day 4

Glad of a rest, though I feel stronger than when I arrived. I think I've learned to make friends for the first time in my life. I don't seem to mind living on top of everyone any more. After all it's the same for all of us.

Day 5

What an end to the holiday! We went canoeing with some experts, and you could hear the water roaring as we paddled out into the river. Then whoosh! down we went, trying to keep upright. Huge rocks rushed past us, and if we were in danger, we never had time to think about it, we were screaming with excitement. Then suddenly we were spinning round in a quiet pool off the main river. Wow! We had to trek back up again, and the 'experts' made us carry the canoes. But it was worth it.

Day 6

Nothing much to say. We left early in the truck. Everyone was sad to go back to our world of comfort. We've learned such a lot about ourselves.

Read the programme for six days at the Lahjung Adventure Centre. Then read Patchara's diary of a class holiday there. Imagine you are Patchara. Miss Ishida has asked you to write an article for your school magazine, in which you:

- express your feelings about your adventure holiday now that it is all over
- try to persuade other students at your school to take part next year.

Base your article on the material in the diary. You should write 1–2 sides, allowing for the size of your handwriting.

[20 marks]

Student E's answer

For my class holiday I visited the Lahjung Adventure Centre, for six days. It was a fantastic experience now that I look back and I am ever so grateful to have been able to encounter such an adventure.

It is hard to get accustomed to the surroundings during the first days, yet it is these surroundings which create the whole atmosphere of adventure. There is no other adventure holiday like this one. It was full of fun, excitement and happiness. What more could you ask for? I made so many new friends and developed a close bonding with them and also with the teachers too, as it is these people which you rely on.

The areas in which we visited were of immense beauty. The waterfall was marvellous and ever so beautiful. Also throughout the jungle trek I came across fasinating mammals, birds and vegetation. Despite this natural beauty it was to my horror when it was brought to my attention that these areas are currently in danger of being destroyed or felled! That is why I feel that you must all try to see and experience these areas of immense beauty before they are destroyed and gone forever.

Visiting the Lahjung Adventure Centre is not only great fun with constant activity and laughter, yet a learning experience too. Throughout the holiday I learned ever so much about who I am as a person. I learned how to make friends and how to help and work together with others. We all bonded and encouraged each other so much that I even felt sad when it all came to an end and I was not the only one!

If you can enjoy making new friends, taking part in once in a lifetime sports and just generally having a great time, then you should defanitely take part next year. I promise you, you will not regret it whatsoever. This Adventure makes you realise just how priveledged we are here today. You learn to live together as one – as a community – yet at the same time take part in breathtaking and daring sports like canoeing down the rapids and rock climbing. So go on, take part next year and see for yourselves just how great this adventure is! I had the best time of my life, you can too.

Student F's answer

I am writing this article to tell you a bit about the class holiday we had at the Lahjung Adventure Centre.

The first day we drove off to the centre. The way there was not very good so the truck pushed us around a lot. The journey there wasn't very comfortable but thinking back it wasn't that bad and it was definetly worth it. When we got there the weather wasn't very pleasant, it was really humid. We were all really shocked when we saw our living conditions. We all had to live so close together and the beds were hard but I suppose it was just getting us prepared for the activities. This reminded me life really was like.

The second day we went rock climbing. I got stuck half way up but even though it was humiliating it was worth every second. When we got up to the top we walked to the most amazing, spectacular, fantastic waterfall I have ever seen and probably will see. It was so amazing.

The third day we went jungle-trekking which was great fun! We got to see lots of different animals and plants. Then when found out later that that part of the jungle might be felled which was upsetting.

All the rest of the days were great fun too.

Now that it's all over I wish I could do it again. I also regret being so negative the first days there because in the end it was great fun.

25

We have learned to not take things for granted and we all have learned how to make friends. These were very useful things to learn.

This trip has made me a better person and I would definatly reccommend all of you to go next year.

Have you ever missed out on something, which everyone else thought was fun? Well then I suggest you go on this amazing, fun, interesting trip. I wouldn't miss it for the world and would definatly go again!

Answer guide When marking both students' work you should think about the following:

- How well is the article presented for the benefit of other students? Does it address them personally? Is it done by implication? Is the tone self-indulgent?
- Look for the use of persuasion.
- Expect a greater weight of narration to comment/evaluation from weaker students.
- Students should cover themes of physical toughening, social awareness, teamwork, overcoming fear and ecological understanding – all from the diary.
- Better students review feelings in retrospect.

Band	Marks	Criteria for content
1	13–15	A confident grasp of themes and issues. Students sift material from the diary efficiently and use a great deal of what is relevant. There is strong development of positive features of the holiday and (usually) analysis of Patchara's change of heart. Comment and evaluation are integrated into much of the article and there is a sense of audience
2	10–12	Material well developed. Students understand the material well and use much of what is relevant. The article has some interesting detail and the ideas are developed, not repeated. Some positive points are explained in favour of the holiday
3	7–9	Competent use of material. Information in the diary is used competently, although there is some mechanical repetition of events. Evaluation and comment is adequate although it may be confined to a separate section at the end and tend towards the general
4	4–6	Some selection of material. The material is rather thinly used, lacking some of the detail that would make the article come alive. Evaluation is attempted, but makes few points
5	1–3	A limited answer. The article makes little helpful use of the material and may not be coherent or particularly relevant. Evaluation is weak or non-existent
6	0	Insufficient material to be placed in Band 5

Band	Marks	Criteria for written expression: structure and persuasive style
1	5	Structure strong, progressive; links; good introduction. Persuasive style argues point
2	4	Structure progressive, non-repetitive. Style persuasive in places
3	3	Structure adequate; ordinary introduction. Style mostly plain
4	2	Structure and sequence inconsistent. Style lacks conviction
5	1	Structure lacks cohesion. Style faulty in places

How to improve your answers

1 Read the question carefully

The examiner will give you all of your directions in the question. It is very important that you read it *slowly* and *carefully* so that you don't miss anything.

Whilst you read, get into the habit of noting down the directions. For example:

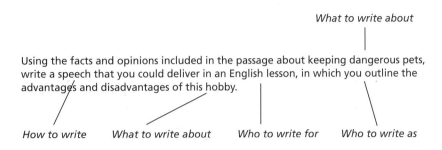

What to write about

Using the facts and opinions included in the passage about keeping dangerous pets, write a speech that you could deliver in an English lesson, in which you outline the advantages and disadvantages of this hobby.

How to write   What to write about   Who to write for   Who to write as

Try this Copy the example questions below and underline, highlight or annotate each one to clarify *exactly* what you are being asked to do.

1 You are Bertalan. Use the notes he made about the end of term concert to write a review of it for the school magazine.

2 Write a dialogue between two scientists at a conference on genetically modified foods in which they discuss their views on the subject. Use the material from the passage to provide two opposing viewpoints.

3 Imagine that you are Ashley's brother or sister. Use what you have read about his year abroad as the basis of a letter in which you explore the possible options for your own 'year off'.

2 Do what you are asked to do

It is important that when you are writing you *make clear* to the examiner that you are doing what you were asked. You must show:

a) who you are writing as

b) who you are writing for

c) that you are writing in a specific style

d) that you have read the passage and have used it as the basis of your writing.

a) Show who you are writing as

- Match your language to the type of person you are writing as. If you are writing as yourself, be very careful to show the examiner your best use of English. Choose a range of vocabulary and make sure it is accurately used, even if it is informal! If you are writing in role, you are not expected to be able to use the vocabulary and dialect of the individual from the passage but you should be able to make a judgement about the level of formality required.
- Include small details about the life and experiences of the character you are writing as. Try to find these in the passage. If there are none then you can make up some as long as you don't waste too much time and they 'fit' your character.

• If you are writing as a character from a passage, always reflect in your writing the personality and attitudes that (s)he showed in the passage. Be careful not to ignore obvious information in the passage, such as gender, age and nationality.

● **Try this**   The passage below is taken from a short story called *The Fury*. It describes a wife who is jealous of the time her husband spends with his pet rabbits.

Before you read it, copy the table on page 29 and then, as you are reading, note down any points that help you to form an impression of Mrs Fletcher.

There were times when Mrs Fletcher was sure her husband thought more of his rabbits than anything else in the world: more than meat and drink, more than tobacco and comfort, more than her – or the other woman. And this was one of those times, this Saturday morning as she looked out from the kitchen where she was preparing the dinner to where she could see Fletcher working absorbedly, cleaning out the hutches, feeding the animals, and grooming his two favourite Angoras for the afternoon's show in Cressley.

She was a passionate woman who clung single-mindedly to what was hers, and was prepared to defend her rights with vigour. While courting Fletcher she had drawn blood on an erstwhile rival who had threatened to reassert her claims. Since then she had had worse things to contend with. Always, it seemed to her, there was something between her and her rightful possession of Fletcher. At the moment it was the rabbits. The big shed had been full of hutches at one time, but now Fletcher concentrated his attention on a handful of animals in which he had a steady faith. But there were still far too many for Mrs Fletcher, who resented sharing him with anything or anybody, and the sight of his absorption now stirred feelings which brought unnecessary force to bear on the sharp knife with which she sliced potatoes for the pan.

'Got a special class for Angoras today,' Fletcher said later, at the table. He was in a hurry to be off and he shovelled loaded spoons of jam sponge pudding into his mouth between the short sentences. 'Might do summat for a change. Time I had a bit o' luck.' He was washed and clean now, his square, ruddily handsome face close-shaven, the railway porter's uniform discarded for his best grey worsted. The carrying-case with the rabbits in it stood by the door.

Mrs Fletcher gave no sign of interest. She said, 'D'you think you'll be back in time for t'pictures?'

Fletcher gulped water. He had a way of drinking which showed his fine teeth. 'Should be,' he answered between swallows. 'Anyway, if you're so keen to go why don't you fix up with Mrs Sykes?'

'I should be able to go out with you, Saturday nights,' Mrs Fletcher said. 'Mrs Sykes has a husband of her own to keep her company.'

'Fat lot o' company he is Saturday night,' Fletcher said dryly. 'Or Sunday, for that matter ... Anyway, I'll try me best. Can't say fairer than that, can I?'

'Not as long as you get back in time.'

Fletcher pushed back in his chair and stood up. 'I don't see why not. It shouldn't be a long job today. It isn't a big show. I should be back by half-past seven at latest.'

'Well, just see 'at you are,' she said.

She stood by the window and watched him go down the road in the pale sunshine, carrying-case, slung from one shoulder, prevented from jogging by a careful hand. He cut a handsome, well-set-up figure when he was dressed up, she thought. Often too handsome, too well-set-up for her peace of mind.

By half-past seven she was washed, dressed, and lightly made-up ready for the evening out. But Fletcher had not returned. And when the clock on the mantleshelf chimed eight there was still no sign of him. It was after ten when he came. She was sitting by the fire, the wireless blaring unheard, her knitting needles flashing with silent fury.

Type of language	Details of her life	Her personality	Her attitudes

You could use these details in your writing to convince the examiner that you were writing as Mrs Fletcher.

b) Be aware of your audience

- Address your audience directly if appropriate.
- Match your language to the type of person you are writing for.
- Select the ideas, detail and examples from the passage that will appeal to the interests and tastes of your audience.

c) Show that you are writing in a specific style

Not all forms of writing are used in directed writing tasks. Here are some that often are:

> **Letter** *Diary* **Newspaper report** **REPORT**
>
> **Speech** *Narrative* Script Review

Each of these forms has a different set of 'ingredients' or rules that make them unique. These are sometimes called conventions. Always use the conventions of the style in which you are writing. Some conventions are to do with:

- how your piece of writing will look; for instance, we all know that newspaper articles are written in columns
- the way that the piece of writing will be organised; for instance, we all know that an essay starts with an introduction and ends with a conclusion
- the kind of information that the piece of writing will contain; for instance, we all know that a newspaper article answers the so-called Five Ws – *Who? Where? When? What? Why?*

● Try this Do you know the conventions for each form of writing set as directed writing tasks?

Copy and complete the table below. The first section has been done for you. (You may wish to use the writing section of this Guide and your IGCSE textbooks to help you.)

Form	Ingredients
Letter	<ul><li>Starts with a greeting</li><li>Ends with a farewell</li><li>First paragraph usually explains purpose of letter</li><li>If formal, uses no slang or colloquial language</li><li>If informal, can use slang and colloquial expression</li><li>Is paragraphed to show a sense of order and development</li></ul>
Diary	
Newspaper report	
Report	
Speech	
Narrative	
Script	
Review	

d) i) **Show that you have used the passage as the basis of your writing**

View the text you have been given as a *source*:

- Write only about events/ideas/attitudes that are included in the passage.
- Use only examples and details from the passage.

The question is your guide. It tells you *what* to write about. Always use it to create a planning grid before you start writing your answer.

Sample question Imagine that you are writing an article for your school magazine about travelling to school safely. Use the ideas and details found in Passages A and B to explore the problems with safe travel and possible solutions.

Sample planning grid

Information to find	Passage A	Passage B
What are the problems?		
What are the causes of the problems?		
What are the solutions?		

● **Try this** Read the following two example questions and produce a planning grid for each one.

1 Using ideas and examples taken from Passages F and G write a dialogue between a teacher and pupil discussing the plans for the end-of-term celebrations, showing their different requirements and opinions.

2 Write a letter to the author of a newspaper article, discussing your views about what makes a good holiday.

Once you have a planning grid drawn up, you are ready to skim read the passage(s) given and pick out basic information which you can include in your writing.

Below is a passage and an exam-type question with a completed planning grid.

Childhood has changed

Dietary characteristics are formed in childhood. As someone who grew up during the 1960s and 1970s I am well aware how childhood has changed. There have been two destructive drivers:

1 Children now are far less active; they are driven to and from school, parents are nervous about them playing outside, there are so many TV channels, computer games, etc.

2 Many families exist solely on processed, ready made meals, fast foods, snack foods and other convenience foods. There are few families which do not include a significant number of these items in their daily diets.

The inevitable has come to pass; more calories are going in, fewer being burnt off; we are getting fatter, very quickly. Though both drivers are equally important the purpose of this article is to deal with the latter.

The problem isn't just one of obesity. Our high fat, high salt, high sugar, high additives diet is lacking in most essential minerals and nutrients. For example, 50 per cent of teenage boys and virtually all teenage girls have intakes of iron less than the UK's Department of Health's recommended level.

Iron deficiency causes anaemia and is linked to key aspects of brain function affecting attention, memory and learning. Intakes of zinc, essential fatty acids and most vitamins are also worryingly absent. There is growing evidence linking deficiency in these vitamins and minerals with a range of conditions including ADHD, dyslexia and autism.

continued

A number of studies directly link diet to behaviour. One of the most significant was carried out at a UK Young Offenders' prison in 2002. The study found that those given vitamin, mineral and essential fatty acid supplements had a 25 per cent reduction in general offending behaviour and a 40 per cent fall in serious offending and violent conduct.

A study at Appleton High School, Wisconsin, showed dramatic improvements in behaviour, quality of working life for teachers and students, and attainment after junk food vending machines were removed and additive free, healthy meal options introduced.

What needs to be done?

1 Remove junk food vending machines – the average fizzy drink is 40 per cent sugar.
2 Replace the junk food in school tuck shops with fruit and other healthy options.
3 Radically reorganise the lunchtime experience by:

a) reducing choice, especially in primary schools where children are often confused by too much choice and, despite knowing what's healthy, choose the wrong option;
b) increasing the amount of fresh food in school meals and where possible buying local and organic;
c) changing the environment – have cloths on tables, real crockery (yes real crockery!), give older children responsibility to eat with and encourage younger ones, etc;
d) seriously invest in school meals, including raising the amount spent on food per meal, which currently averages 36p!

4 Have water bottles in all classrooms.
5 Make cookery and related home economics part of the secondary curriculum.
6 Prohibit all forms of marketing aimed at children, including schemes that link purchases of junk food to school equipment. ★

Sample question Imagine that you and a friend are discussing making changes to the food available at school. One of you agrees with the ideas put forward by the writer, one of you does not. Write the script of your conversation, making sure that you cover the following topics:
a) What can be done?
b) Why is change needed?

Sample planning grid

What can be done?	Why is change needed?	Friend's view
Less choice	Children will always make the wrong choices/get confused	It's our right to eat what we want to
More fresh food, less junk	Will improve • health – obesity/iron • learning/memory • behaviour/attention At home there's too much convenience food	• Not the school's business • Won't make any difference once per day • Whole lifestyle needs to change, e.g. exercise
Better environment		What's that got to do with health?
Higher quality/cost	Only 36p per meal is spent at present in the UK	Where will the money come from?
Water in class		
Cookery on curriculum	It will teach us all about healthy eating even if our families don't	I'm too busy to waste my time on cookery
Ban marketing aimed at children	Some foods are seen as cool – this is hard for children to fight	Rubbish – only idiots think food is cool

● **Try this** For many older people, overseas travel and volunteering provides both a challenge and a chance to offer help where it can do most good. What's more, it's a world where experience counts.

Alive: A gap in your life?

It isn't only for students. An ever-growing number of thirtysomethings are giving up career and even home for travel, fun and adventure, writes Claire Sawers

By the time Clare and Graham Laybourne reached their early thirties they had settled into a comfortable routine. The professional couple owned a spacious flat in Edinburgh, enjoyed well-paid jobs and an affluent lifestyle.

Work didn't leave much time for their shared passion of hillwalking, but whenever possible they squeezed in a short break.

Sometimes, though, it wasn't enough. Late at night the couple would idly debate giving it all up to go trekking in Nepal or New Zealand. It was something they had always dreamt of, but careers, bills and a mortgage got in the way.

However, the idea wouldn't go away. Waiting until retirement was not an option for such a physically demanding trip. And if they put it off much longer their financial commitments would only multiply.

So two years ago Clare and Graham took the plunge. They resigned from their jobs – Clare, 32, was a lawyer and Graham, 36, a financial manager – and sold their flat. They threw a farewell party for friends and family, withdrew their savings from the bank and set off in a second-hand car crammed with hiking gear.

"It was pretty scary, but we thought, 'This is our opportunity, we have to take it'," says Clare.

In the course of a year the couple climbed the Alps, hiked across Corsica, explored Yosemite national park in California and spent two months trekking with a sherpa in the Nepalese mountains.

With the exception of a beach stopover in Thailand where they chilled out in the sun, the action was nonstop, ending with a campervan tour of Australia and New Zealand.

"It was just the most amazing experience," says Clare from her newfound suburban bolt hole in Colinton, Edinburgh. "We both really appreciated the freedom and escape from stress. We were very lucky to have been able to afford it financially. It was such a luxury to take time out like that."

Had Clare and Graham embarked on their travels when 10 years younger they would have been typical backpackers. But having waited until their careers were established, then setting off with more than loose change from a student loan in their pockets, the couple are what the travel industry has dubbed flashpackers.

This growing new breed of traveller is just as free-spirited as gap-year students and shares their yearning to discover new places. But much as they enjoy a challenge, flashpackers also relish having the money to occasionally splash out on room service in a four-star hotel instead of handing over a few baht for a spartan beach hut and a bowl of rice.

A survey by the guidebook publisher Lonely Planet revealed that the average student gap year trip costs about £3,000, compared to £6,000 for older travellers. As well as opting for more comforts than the younger traveller, flashpackers pack decent clothes, credit cards and high-tech gadgets.

Stowed inside their designer luggage is everything from a digital camera, mobile phone with camera for chatting with friends back home, camcorder and iPod. Rather than record details of their trip in a dog-eared notebook, they will create a travel blog and post it on the internet for anyone to read.

Last year alone, an estimated 200,000 British travellers, with an average age of 32, bought round-the-world tickets. That figure is expected to rise further this year. Favourite destinations include Australia, Chile, Brazil and New Zealand.

The trend towards grown-up gap years prompted Lonely Planet to publish a special guide catering for their travel needs. The Career Break Book points out that gap years, once the preserve of students and restless twentysomethings, are now also open to professionals. It urges readers to "Swap your briefcase for a passport and live your dream."

Joe Bindloss, a contributing author, says many thirtysomethings feel a gap year represents their last chance to do something genuinely liberating and exciting. "For some it's about fulfilling a lifelong ambition while you can afford to make the necessary sacrifices.

"For others it's a desire to step off the treadmill and amass really interesting and valuable experience in a foreign place."

Jamie Wallace, a 31-year-old engineer from Aberdeen, decided to work a season in a French ski resort after he was made redundant. "I had spent a lot of time working really long hours and felt I was missing out on the good stuff. When I lost my job, I had the cash, and no real ties to hold me back, so I just left," he said.

After working and playing hard in Val d'Isere, Wallace caught up with friends living in Spain, and travelled through Europe for several months. "I didn't take a gap year to 'find myself'," he says with a laugh. "It was more about grabbing the chance to have a bit of responsibility-free fun before I started looking for my next job."

His sentiments echo many of those taking a career break, says Bindloss. "There's been a shift in attitudes and lots of people take a year out to redress the work/life balance thing. Us Brits are famous for working far longer hours than our European counterparts, and now we want to put family or leisure time further up the list of priorities."

Sam Withall, a businesswoman with three children, decided to take her family abroad after a particularly stressful period at work. She and her husband, Toby, and their children – Barney, 9, Arthur, 7 and four-year-old Eliza – travelled through India, Vietnam, Thailand, Australia, New Zealand and the United States.

Withall, 39, who runs clothing stores in Edinburgh, Perth and St Andrews, missed out on a gap year first time round. "I was just getting fed up. I'd been working for myself for 12 years and realised I wasn't spending enough time with my kids," she says.

The family alternated between expensive hotels and sleeping in a campervan. "It was incredible to spend all that time together. At home, Toby and I used to argue a lot. When we were away, we had such a laugh," says Withall.

"The whole trip probably cost between £25,000 and £30,000. It's a huge cost, but then again some people may spend that on a new kitchen," she says.

"Before I went I would probably have wanted 10 shops and a bigger house. Since we've been home we're thinking about moving to St Andrews and spending more time as a family."

Clare Laybourn also believes that being away from work has given her a fresh perspective. "Now, when I have a bad day at work, or am stressing about a pay rise or something, I think of the people we met in Nepal. They had really hard lives and were so incredibly kind. It really helps," she says.

Catherine Raynor, of Voluntary Service Overseas, which attracts a growing number of thirty- and fortysomething professionals seeking a change of pace and culture, agrees that a gap year can bring much-needed focus to a jaded worker's life.

continued

VSO works in partnership with several employers, including Shell, BT and Pricewaterhouse Coopers, to arrange placements in such developing countries as Ethiopia or Tanzania. Staff are given a salary, flights and pension scheme, and are guaranteed a job on return.

"This way employees can live their dream, take time out, and come back feeling more resourceful and able to work under pressure," says Raynor. "For companies, it's actually a staff retention tool."

And for those who make the leap, the rewards of travelling add up to more than a pay rise or company pension.

"The only bad thing about it has been coming back and feeling very unsettled. Your values change when you are away, but sometimes they are the changes you need," said Withall.

Imagine that one of your parents is thinking about travelling and working overseas with a volunteer programme. Using ideas from the passage write a letter in which you point out:

a) the positives to be gained from doing volunteer work
b) the negatives of doing volunteer work.

Draw up and complete a planning grid for this question:

Positives	Negatives

d) ii) Show that you have used precise details as the basis of your writing

The examiner will be looking for detail to be included in your writing. You must be careful to use only detail from the text, otherwise your work becomes creative writing!

To avoid using your imagination instead of the text, think of every paragraph you write as a plant, with an idea from the text as its root and details from the text as its stem. You can make up some additional, but relevant, detail to be its flower.

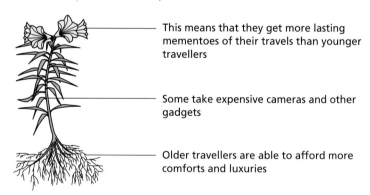

This means that they get more lasting mementoes of their travels than younger travellers

Some take expensive cameras and other gadgets

Older travellers are able to afford more comforts and luxuries

● **Try this** Find two more points from the passage about travelling and overseas volunteer work. Select some detail and add your own detail to create a fully developed 'plant'.

Key revision points
- Understand that directed writing is a test of reading and writing.
- Read and analyse the question before reading the passage.
- When reading the passage, complete a planning grid.
- When writing your answer, focus on who you are writing *as*, who you are writing *for* and in which *form* you are writing.
- When writing your answer, always include ideas with detail from the passage.

TOPIC 5 Summary writing tasks

Key objectives

- To make sure that you understand what summary writing is
- To help you to understand the way that summary writing is marked by examiners
- To make sure that you understand the common mistakes that students make when tackling summary writing tasks
- To revise key strategies for approaching summary writing tasks

Key definition

Term	Definition
Summary writing	To sum up means to condense a text without losing important information, so writing a summary involves taking the essential meaning from what you read, but making it shorter

Key ideas

Summary writing is where the examiner is *directing* you about:

- what part of the text to summarise
- how to organise your summary
- how much to write
- how to write.

Common misconceptions and errors

Some students approach the summary question on an IGCSE examination paper as if it were a precis. In fact, the type of summary you will be asked to complete is a selective summary where you are asked to pick out specific facts or content as opposed to summarising the whole text. The number of texts that you have to read to find this information will depend upon whether you are taking the Core or Extended paper. Core candidates read one passage only; Extended candidates read two. ■

Some students think that their actual writing – paragraphing, spelling and grammar – does not matter in summary writing. This is not strictly true. The clarity, concision and organisation of your writing will affect your writing marks and can even affect your reading marks as it may not be possible for the examiner to identify the original point if your expression is poor. ■

Some students think that summary writing is based on ideas from their imagination or on their opinions on a given topic. This is a dangerous misconception and can lead to a very low mark being awarded. ■

Some students include examples and quotations from the passage. These are not necessary. ■

Sample question and answers

Sample question Read Passages A and B. Summarise the type of preparations made for natural disasters in America and the effects of such events.

A Reporters' Logs: Katrina's aftermath

2 September 2005: Thousands of people are stranded in New Orleans without food or water after Hurricane Katrina – a fierce mass of winds swirling at 155mph (250km/h) – caused widespread devastation to the region.

President Bush is visiting the area after acknowledging the initial response was "not acceptable" and pledged to restore order in the city.

BBC correspondents report on the latest developments from the worst-hit areas of Louisiana and Mississippi.

Bill Turnbull: Biloxi, LA: 09:26 GMT

What is extraordinary about this storm is its unimaginable power.

There are so many objects that have been picked up and thrown to the ground as if by an angry child. There is a generator next to a car. There is also some kind of straw mattress. An office chair. There are some paper cups on the ground. And there is some kind of waste paper bin. And then just above it a motorbike.

Around the corner in Biloxi's Hayes Street, I met some neighbours taking stock of their new situation. I ask them what they are doing now.

A man tells me, "We're just taking it one day at a time. It's all we can do. I've got about five inches of mud in the house. The appliances are all ruined, the clothes, everything. All destroyed." I ask him and his friends sitting with him if they have had any help from the authorities yet. "No. All they have been doing is patrolling this area and that's it."

"They are trying to feed the people in the shelters. Giving them oxygen and stuff but we are hungry too," another man says.

"I understand that but I believe they should have more mobility. They should help more people rather than dealing with certain sections. Everybody needs help," his friend says.

And if you are here in Biloxi you do need help.

We found Sharon on a lonely road. She was still looking for lost friends. "This is terrible. It's terrible man. It's the aftermath, man. The reality has set in. It is just too much." I wish her good luck and hope she stays safe.

She says thank you.

Jamie Coomarasamy: Baton Rouge, LA : 06:45 GMT

With every day the level of desperation here is rising. Thousands of people are still trapped inside New Orleans in a city where the authorities appear overwhelmed by the scale of the disaster.

Like many of the people living in unsanitary and dangerous conditions in the city, local officials are now pointing fingers, in their case at the federal government.

The head of New Orleans emergency operations described the relief effort as a national disgrace. He asked why America can send massive amounts of aid to tsunami victims but can't bail out his city.

Meanwhile, thousands of national guardsmen are due to arrive in Louisiana from across the United States to try to stem a tide of lawlessness which threatens to leave scars on the community long after the floodwaters have receded.

B Beat the quake, man

This article describes the procedures that minimise damage and loss of life when an earthquake occurs in the USA

April in California is earthquake preparedness month. Around two million people state wide scramble under desks and tables at 10.10 in the morning on the first of the month in a special 'Duck, cover and hold' drill to kick things off. The rest of April is set aside for various theme weeks – business awareness, home awareness, school awareness, etc. The month's mascot, a groovy sunglasses-wearing cartoon creature in the shape of California, holds aloft a wrench and advises 'Beat the quake! Bolt it, brace it, fasten it down!'

Such is life in the San Francisco Bay Area, where over five million people live and work astride two very active fault lines. Everyone knows the quakes are out there somewhere since the US Geological Survey has mapped everything extensively and can forecast probabilities with reasonable accuracy. The question is, what to do about it. The philosophy which has changed the state's thinking lies along the lines of preventative dentistry – damage is most easily fixed before it occurs.

Richard Eisner is the director of the Bay Area Regional Earthquake Preparedness Project (BAREPP), a branch of California's Office of Emergency Services (OES). 'Outside this country there is tremendous life loss where construction uses local materials and is not carried out professionally,' he says. 'But here we had earthquake building codes in use throughout the state, after the Long Beach quake in 1933.'

As a result, all public schools, hospitals, fire and police stations – those structures designated as 'essential services' – must pass a state design review and be constructed to withstand a quake. Additional codes since the 1971 San Fernando quake have set minimum standards for almost every type of building.

BAREPP's preparedness measures include a large dose of educational activities – hence the cartoon humanoid with the wrench. 'For a number of years now our emphasis has been on developing skills,' says Eisner; 'on getting people to be able to fend for themselves for the vital first 72 hours. We have been telling people not to depend on the government for anything. For that period of time we're basically an underdeveloped country.'

Of course the real test of any plan is the actual event you've been planning for. The Loma Prieta quake, 7.1 on the Richter scale, which struck south of the Bay Area in 1989, had been much planned for. A survey of the area had determined there was a high probability of a quake within thirty years and had indicated which areas would be most vulnerable to damage. A simulated earthquake drill had been conducted three months before.

Reaction to the quake was quick. At undamaged Candlestick Park, where the third game of baseball's World Series had been getting under way, no one was really sure what had happened, although one sports announcer dug out the phone book and started reading the earthquake instructions over the radio. Over in the state capitol the OES people went scrambling for their State Operations Centre, where they began putting together a picture of what had happened and figured out who needed what. The phones were working so faxes were soon flying, sending out press releases and enabling resources to be co-ordinated. With a few exceptions, local police and firefighting rescue teams were able to handle emergencies in their own areas without need of assistance since their buildings were intact and the roads and hospitals usable. The 27 000-strong National Guard was on alert within 20 minutes and soon on its way to provide shelter, food and water to those in cut-off areas.

The final Loma Prieta statistics – 62 dead, 3,757 injured and six billion dollars in damage – pale in comparison to the havoc wreaked by the earthquake in Armenia the year before, which was of similar magnitude but which killed 25 000 people.

Answer guide

Content

Preparations before and after the disaster happens	Effects that the disaster has on people/places
1 The authorities make children/parents/businesses *aware* of how to deal with natural disasters	1 Death and injury to the population
2 People practise ('duck, cover and hold') drills	2 People are in danger; trapped in damaged and unsafe buildings
3 People learn to survive on their own (for 72 hours); do not rely on the state	3 Friends and family cannot be found
4 Building codes in force; minimum standards for buildings, materials	4 Homes and personal possessions are ruined; mud and debris in buildings; many people are made homeless
5 'Essential service' buildings (examples) especially strong; must pass special tests	5 Widespread devastation
6 Forecasts made of when disasters are likely	6 Objects have been relocated by the force of the disaster
7 When there is a disaster, those in charge react immediately	7 There are no essentials available; no help, food, water
8 Resources are well co-ordinated	8 Shelters are set up for those made homeless and in need of help
9 Police/firefighters/national guard do their duty immediately	9 Aid is directed at the official shelters only (not to any other places)
10 They provide essentials (shelter, food, water) for the victims	10 The authorities are overwhelmed
	11 Conditions are unsanitary and pose a serious health risk
	12 People are angry at the delays in aid
	13 Lawlessness and disorder breaks out

Give 1 mark for any of these points reasonably clearly expressed, up to a maximum of 15 marks.

Quality of writing

Band	Marks	Criteria
1	5	All points are made clearly and concisely in the student's own words. The answer is strongly focused on the passages and on the question
2	4	Most of the answer is concise and well focused even if there is an inappropriate introduction. Own words are used consistently
3	3	There are some examples of concision. There may be occasional loss of focus. Own words are used
4	2	The answer is mostly focused but there may be examples of comment, repetition or unnecessarily long explanation. There may be occasional copying
5	1	The answer frequently loses focus and is wordy. There may be frequent copying
	0	Over-reliance on copying; insufficient focus to be placed in Band 5

Student's answer

Preparations

A powerful country like the United States can spend a lot on preparing themselves for natural disasters. The measures taken to decrease the human risk include education in the procedures taken in the event if a natural disaster, such as getting under the desk and assuming the 'braced' position. The USA also makes efforts to predict natural disasters in order to prepare and evacuate people as much as possible. Another precaution take is the way in which the build the cities themselves. Building codes exist which set a standard of safety in all buildings, rendering them more earthquake proof.

Effects

The preparations made for natural disasters stand the USA in much better stead than many LEDCs. They are unable, however, to completely safeguard themselves. Once the disaster has occurred emergency services, despite their resources, cannot necessarily reach everybody on time. Although there is a human cost, it is much lower then that of LEDCs and the losses for the USA are generally more economic.

Examiner's comments

Although this student may have understood the passages quite well, the answer is too short to show this and is unbalanced with more information from one passage than the other.

Main issues to note about this answer are:

- *The answer is clearly organised into the two parts of the question, although headings are not necessary.*
- *The answer misses the opportunity to make the range of points possible about preparations and makes only one point about effects leaving it unbalanced and too short.*
- *There is no specific reference to the first passage at all.*
- *Time is wasted with general preambles such as "Another precaution is the way in which the(y) build the cities themselves."*

Overall this makes brief reference to each passage (Preparations 1,6,5, Effects 10) and fits into Band 4 for writing producing a total of (4 + 2) 6 marks.

Student's answer The best preparation is to forecast what might happen in advance so everyone can get out or be ready. Also in California people practise routines for earthquakes, where to go in an earthquake and what to do. There are methods to make the people of California more aware of earthquakes and there are catchy slogans to keep them interested. In San Francisco building codes have been introduced so buildings will not collapse during earthquakes. Important buildings must be really safe. Simulated earthquake drills are often used to test the cities awareness. The authorities and police have to be ready to help straight away and they have to get plans agreed in advance. In areas which have had preparation many people die but no way near as many as in areas with no preparation.

Many people can be without food or water and can feel angry about the help (food, medicine and water) they get, because it only goes to the shelters and even then it takes too long to arrive. Many people were homeless and with hardly any clothes to wear after the effects of Hurricane Katrina. They couldn't find their families and friends. Trees were uprooted, cars thrown around and belongings lost in the streets. The water was polluted and it got dangerous due to disease and The National Guard were sent to Louisiana to stop the looting which was leaving scars on the economy.

Examiner's comments *This student has understood both of the passages quite well, the answer is of an acceptable length and contains a wide range of points.*
  Main issues to note about this answer are:

- *The answer is clearly organised into the two parts of the question.*
- *The answer makes a range of points about preparations and effects.*
- *Both passages are referred to.*
- *Expression is a little clumsy and imprecise (for instance references to 'hardly any clothes' when the passage states that clothes were ruined) and points are not particularly orderly but repetition is avoided.*

Overall this makes sound reference to each passage (Preparations 6,2,1,4,5,7,9,8, Effects 7,12,9,4,3,6,11,13) and fits into Band 3 for writing producing a total of (15 + 3) 16 marks.

● **Try this**
- Read the passages on pages 41–3 taken from a past exam paper.
- Read the summary writing question set on them.
- Then look at the students' answers that have been provided.
- Look at the answer guide on **page 44**, which the examiner used to mark these responses. What marks would you give? (Answers are given on **page 91**.)

A All rise, here comes the judge

This passage is about a highly experienced yachtsman who is also a lawyer and runs a film-making business

Growing up on an island near Oslo, Norway, Christen Horn Johannessen began sailing when he was five years old. 'I've been sailing smaller boats all my life, but sailing around the world was never my goal,' says the helmsman for the boat *Djuice* in the Volvo Ocean Race. 'I used to say to my friends: "Remind me never to get involved with round-the-world races." I thought those guys were crazy. And now here I am doing it for the second time!' As Grant Wharington, a famous Australian competitor, says, much of the attraction of the Volvo Ocean Race lies in speed. The idea of sailing as fast as or faster than the weather systems or of reaching Cape Horn from Auckland in seven days is exciting. Christen agrees, but points out that there's more to the race than high-speed sailing, saying: 'When you are sitting on the deck at night, there are literally millions of stars above you, and sometimes the ocean is glowing and shining because of the phosphor in the water. You get very close to nature, and moments like these remind you how small you are in the scheme of things, and how lucky we all are to be doing what we do.'

In addition to his sailing duties, Christen is also responsible for on-board media production, filming and still photography. This has the added enjoyment of providing excellent communications between the crew and their families, who are also reunited during stopovers after each leg. On Christen's last trip around the world, he gained an impressive cult following for the hilarious and witty film sequences he and fellow crew member Nick Willetts sent out to the world from the Innovation Kvcerner boat, which finished fourth.

Together, the two sailors formed the company Snus Korp Productions, which is still in operation. However, Nick is not with the *Djuice* crew this time, so he operates his part of the company from his home in Australia. The position in front of the camera on board *Djuice* is yet to be filled by one of the new members of the crew. Christen says: 'We have four cameras permanently mounted on the boat and two hand-held cameras, one of them on 24 hours a day. It's not only a question of public relations – we really want to share our experience with other people. Besides, everyone enjoys being the star for a while in front of the camera.' Christen knows of course that the race is not just about being a media star. Much of the satisfaction of taking part is in planning and executing strategies and in finding out whether they work or not. The correct choice of a route after studying currents and weather patterns can result in gaining great distances on one's fellow competitors.

Christen has a professional life on land that has nothing to do with sailing. When he decided to compete in the last round-the-world race he took a year off from his job as a district court judge. Now he is working as an attorney and has again taken another year off to compete in the Volvo Ocean Race. He says: 'When I sailed my last race, it wasn't long before the crew were all calling me "Judge", but it hasn't helped me a bit on the boat. I have no authority there at all!' He also knows that the race will often be hard and boring: keeping watch, changing sails, going to bed for four hours, and the same again next day, and the next. The real thrill does not lie in watching the ocean but in the things you see on the way, like passing Cape Horn in brilliant sunshine. That really reminds him why he is taking part in the race.

B No ordinary seamen

In this passage, the journalist Libby Purves writes about taking part in a race in an old sailing ship with tall masts. The ship is called Europa *and nearly all the crew are amateurs*

The first night out of Antwerp we eyed each other up. There was a group of Dutch teenagers, each with their own story: fragile, pretty Mienke, shy Vince, bouncy Anouk, who had won her berth in a competition; then a thin Swiss 18-year-old called Anna who had fought juvenile arthritis since she was 10 but was determined to have a go at this voyage; Lisa from New Zealand with a glittering stud in her nose, working her way round Europe; and little Anya, the student teacher from Poland, who arrived breathless in Antwerp the night before we sailed, giving her whole year's savings for the adventure and far from clear about how she would get home from Norway.

The three adult trainees taking a break from real life were myself, Alex from America, and Ingrid, a heavy-set, shy, religious education teacher in her thirties who had never been outside Belgium in her whole life.

The long-term crew told us stories of the Antarctic trip: ice on the rigging, snow on the deck, spray blown so thick over the deck in the Drake Passage that the lookout had to climb the mast. Klaas, the captain, and his mates told us to organise our own rotas for steering and keeping lookout. 'Be nice to each other,' said Erik, the second mate. 'That's important.' We were all apprehensive. The ship was short-handed, so we were divided into two watches only – rotating six hours by day, four hours by night. For ten days, considering mealtimes and all-hands-on-deck calls, none of us would ever sleep more than four hours at a stretch, and that was only once every 24 hours.

The race began. The winds were fair, the sea not particularly rough, but sickness was rife. Most fought it: only one Dutch girl retired to her bunk and refused all week to do anything whatsoever. At the other end of the scale, Anya would stumble on deck sick but smiling, with little bare feet poking out of the bottom of her oilskin trousers. 'This is how I am fighting the seasickness,' she said grandly. 'When my feet feel the deck I am nearly OK.' There was much to induce seasickness.

The unusual standard of comfort on board (cabins of four and six with toilet ensuite) gets *Europa* nicknamed 'the hotel ship' by those who sail in more spartan vessels with hammocks instead of bunks, but there are few hotels where guests wash the galley floor at 2 am, or sew sails in the dawn.

We learn English is the second deck-language on most European ships, and once the Dutch names of sails and lines – *onderbram, grootzeil, fok* – are in your head, it is easy enough to obey orders to carry out a manoeuvre. Less easy to be brave: I was not among those who worked high aloft, and feel some shame because of it.

Here was I, used to the sea on small yachts for 25 years and clad in proper Musto oilskins, out-performed by green, gallant teenagers in chain-store anoraks who hardly knew port from starboard.

So I humbly volunteered for extra duties at the helm and lookout watches when it rained, which it rather frequently did.

At first, tired despite the flying progress of the ship, we fantasised constantly about our bunks. It is pure chilly misery, after a mere half-hour of sleep, to be called on deck because a boom has snapped or a sail blown out, to haul and pack away sails in the icy rain. It is unnerving to watch a North Sea squall come up from behind, a thickening black line sliding over green water, and hear the mate's warning cry 'Take away skysail! Take away bram!' and join the scramble to the lines to get the high sails out of the tearing wind.

Summarise:

a) what you think Christen Horn Johannessen finds enjoyable about taking part in the Volvo Ocean Race

b) what Libby Purves says about the hard work and discomforts of sailing in tall ships.

Write about 1 side in total, allowing for the size of your handwriting.

[20 marks]

Student G's answer

Christen felt lucky to be able to sail; it made a change from his usual job and gave him a chance to make films which was different too. I think he also enjoyed using new skills such as planning strategies to beat the weather and being close to nature which he wouldn't be in his 'day job'! He really liked the things he got to see: stars and beautiful sights as well.

Libby described sailing as uncomfortable. She wrote about the cold, the rain and the strong winds which must make people feel uncomfortable, on top of feeling sea sick! It was also hard work. They had to work outside in the elements for long shifts, sometimes in the night or at weird times, without much sleep. Some of the things they had to do were hard too – like mending sails, washing floors and repairing broken equipment. Sometimes they even had to work up high in the rigging. (158 words)

Student H's answer

I think that Christen really liked sailing and Libby didn't. Maybe that's because she wasn't used to it. And the others were better at it than her. She had awful weather and got sick too but he could look at the nice sights. They both had work to do and he made films which he liked doing because it meant he could keep in touch with people at home. Libby had to work really hard and didn't get much sleep which I think would be very difficult. In the passage she says that one girl just went to her cabin and didn't come out. I might do something like that because I get sick on boats and in cars. I'd be no good at mending things either. (119 words)

43

Answer guide

Content

Passage A	Passage B
1 Beauty of natural objects (stars, phosphor, Cape), i.e. what he sees	**11** Cold – ice and snow
2 Features of landscape (e.g. the Cape)	**12** Long watches; steering; shifts
3 Part of nature; tiny speck; close to nature	**13** Seasickness
4 Privilege, luck to be sailing	**14** Wash floors; sew sails; work at odd hours
5 High speeds (e.g. beating the weather systems)	**15** All have to help repair snapped boom, pack sails
6 Chance to make films, share experience	**16** Working aloft
7 Media star, cult following	**17** Little sleep; weariness
8 Change from work	**18** Might have to sleep in hammocks
9 Work out strategies; see them work	**19** Rain; spray
10 Communicate with families; stopovers	**20** Gales; tearing winds
	21 Extra shifts

Give 1 mark for any of these points, up to a maximum of 15 marks.

Written expression

Band	Marks	Criteria
1	5	All points are made clearly and concisely in the student's own words. The answer is strongly focused on the passages and on the question
2	4	Most of the answer is concise and well focused even if there is an inappropriate introduction. Own words are used consistently
3	3	There are some examples of concision. There may be occasional loss of focus. Own words are used
4	2	The answer is mostly focused but there may be examples of comment, repetition or unnecessarily long explanation. There may be occasional copying from text
5	1	The answer frequently loses focus and is wordy. There may be frequent copying
	0	Over-reliance on copying from text; insufficient focus to be placed in B and 5

How to improve your answers

1 Read the questions carefully

The examiner will direct you to the specific information you are expected to summarise. It is very important that you read the question *slowly* and *carefully* so that you don't miss these specific instructions.

Whilst you read the question, get into the habit of noting down the specific area or areas that you must summarise. The question is your guide. It tells you *what* to write about. The example at the top of the next page shows how you could do this.

*Reasons why boy
doesn't enjoy himself*

Summarise the reasons why the boy does not enjoy spending time with his aunty, as shown in Passage A, and why some carers find charity work difficult, from Passage B.

*Reasons why
carers unhappy*

Always use this to create a planning grid before you start writing your answer.

● **Try this** Copy the example questions below and underline, highlight or annotate each one to clarify exactly what you are being asked to summarise.

1 Read the two passages and summarise the different responses that victims have to serious crime, using both passages.

2 Summarise the reasons that Frederick Gibson gives for enjoying his life as a pianist in Passage A. Summarise the disadvantages of being a professional musician shown in Passage B.

2 Read the passage(s) very carefully

As you read, ask yourself questions, in your mind, about the meaning of different sentences, phrases and words and also about what the writer may be suggesting even if it isn't clearly stated; the ability to identify implied points is one way in which good answers stand out from merely satisfactory ones. Do not rush this reading; it is crucial that you gain as full an understanding of the passage as you can before you begin to write anything.

3 Plan how to organise your summary

Use the question to guide you on the way to organise your answer.

- If the question is subdivided into parts **a)** and **b)** then you should split your answer into parts **a)** and **b)**.
- If the question asks you to select information related to one topic from the two texts then you have a choice. You could deal with the topic in each text separately, or you could focus on one feature at a time and find information about it from both texts and mix this together.
- Always keep a look-out for any points that can be linked with others; you will be given credit for showing that you can *synthesise* ideas and *reorganise* them. You may find it helpful to create a notes grid at this point.

Sample question Summarise the technological innovations that are obvious in the two cities and also the historical features that are still evident.

Sample planning grid

Information to find	Passage A	Passage B
Technological innovations		
Historical features		

● **Try this** Read the following example questions and produce a planning grid for each one.

1 Both passages include a surprising event. How did the children in each passage react to the surprises? Summarise their reactions.

2 The weather created problems and pleasures for the marathon runner in Passage A and the swimmers in Passage B. Summarise the problems and pleasures shown in both passages.

4 Select only material that is relevant

Read the passage(s) carefully, noting relevant points in your grid, or highlighting or underlining all the points that seem to be relevant to the topic about which you will have to write. At the same time, mentally ignore all details that are not directly related to the topic.

5 Keep to the word limit

You will probably be required to write your answer within a stated word limit. Alternatively you may be required to write a certain number of sides of answer paper depending on the size of your handwriting. Be careful to give equal weight to each of your main points as you write; also think about how many words each point should be given. For example, if you have a word limit of 200 words and 10 main points, that is, on average, 20 words per point.

If you go over or under the word limit it is likely that you will not show the skills necessary to gain a high mark for quality of writing.

6 Use your own words as far as possible

Once you have read the passage thoroughly, write down in note form the points you have marked. Make sure these are all related to the main topic of the summary.

When writing your notes try to put the phrases you have marked into your own words. There will be some words which you cannot change without losing their meaning. It is not necessary to find a synonym for every word in the passage. However, if you copy out whole phrases and sentences the examiner does not know whether you have understood the passage or not and this could affect the quality of writing mark that you are given.

7 Show you have used the passage as the basis of your writing

View the text you have been given as a *source* and write only about events/ideas/attitudes that are included in the passage. Never add your own views or examples from your experience.

Key revision points

■ Understand that summary writing is a test of reading and writing.
■ Read and analyse the question before reading the passage.
■ When reading the passage, complete a planning grid.
■ When writing your answer, focus on what you are summarising.
■ When writing your answer, never include your own ideas or quotes but only detail from the passage.

TOPIC 6 Composition skills

Key objectives

- To make sure that you are aware of the different types of continuous writing and of their specific requirements
- To help you understand the ways that continuous writing questions are marked by examiners
- To make sure that you understand the common mistakes that students make when tackling continuous writing tasks under examination conditions
- To suggest ways of preparing yourself to answer continuous writing tasks in the examination

Key definitions

Term	Definition
Register	The distinctive tone in which something is written and which makes the writing fit for its purpose. Register can be either formal or informal and depends on the writer's choice of words, sentence structures, and so on
Audience	The person(s) at whom your writing is directed. The register you choose should be suited to your audience
Context	The framework within which your writing is set. For example, you could be asked to write in the context of a letter to a newspaper, an article for a school magazine, and so on. It is important that the tone and register of your writing is appropriate to the context

How are these skills tested in examinations?

The writing tasks you will be required to do for IGCSE First Language English can be divided into the following main categories:

- argumentative/discursive writing
- descriptive writing
- informative writing
- narrative writing.

If you are taking Component 3 (directed writing and composition), Section 2 requires you to write only one task.

Type of question	Skill 1	Skill 2	Skill 3	Skill 4	Skill 5
	Articulating experience and expressing what is thought, felt and imagined	Ordering and presenting facts, ideas and opinions	Understanding and using a range of appropriate vocabulary	Using language and a register appropriate to audience and context	Making accurate and effective use of paragraphs, grammatical structures, sentences, punctuation and spelling
Argumentative writing	✔	✔	✔	✔	✔
Discursive writing	✔	✔	✔	✔	✔
Descriptive writing		✔	✔	✔	✔
Narrative writing	✔		✔	✔	✔
Informative writing		✔	✔	✔	✔

Key ideas

As you can see from these five key skills, the organisation of your writing is very important. How do you approach planning and organising your work? Here are some points to consider.

Ordering and presenting facts, ideas and opinions

Planning your writing

- Never start to write before you have thought about what you are going to say.
- Always make a plan to help you put your ideas into the best order.
- The sort of plan you make is up to you – you may like to make a skeleton plan or a mind map or a simple numbered list of points. Choose the approach with which you, personally, are happiest.
- Your plan should not be too long (especially under examination conditions); there's nothing to be gained from writing out your whole essay in rough and then rewriting it again neatly!
- Openings and endings are particularly important as they create good or bad impressions on the reader: get them clear in your mind before you start to write. The opening should give a clear indication of the direction your writing is going to take and your ending should be clearly signalled. There's a great difference between a piece of writing that reaches a considered ending and one that just stops!
- Once you have made your plan, stick to it (especially when you're under examination conditions).
- Relate the points in the plan to the title about which you're writing.
- Once you have made a list of the main points of your writing then you need to think about organising them into a coherent whole. Where do you start? It's a good idea to have the conclusion of your writing in your mind as an objective to work towards – especially with an argumentative or discursive essay.
- Next put your points in order; each main point will form the topic sentence of each of your paragraphs.

Making accurate and effective use of paragraphs

- Your writing must be organised into paragraphs.
- Each paragraph should be structured around a topic sentence.
- A topic sentence is the sentence that conveys the main point of your paragraph. It usually comes at the start of the paragraph but could also come at the middle or end.
- Putting the topic sentence in different places in different paragraphs gives variety to your writing which is something examiners will reward.

- Using topic sentences as the basis for a skeleton plan for your essay is a good way to organise your ideas.
- Each paragraph should follow on logically from the one before it and lead logically into the one that follows it.

● **Try this** Here are some example topic sentences. Develop a paragraph around each of them. Remember that the topic sentence does not have to be the opening sentence of a paragraph.

a) She mounted her bicycle and quickly rode away from the scene.

b) The clothes you wear say a lot about your personality.

c) I waited, becoming increasingly more worried, but no-one appeared.

d) My new friend has some very strange habits.

e) Some people like to spend their free time watching television.

Understanding and using a range of appropriate vocabulary

The examination requires you to show that you can use a range of varied and appropriate vocabulary. Let's look at ways in which you can approach this.

- It is important that you choose your words carefully in order to convey precise shades of meaning to your readers.
- Try to be sensitive to the different connotations of the words you use. For example, think about the different shades of meaning in the words *kill, murder, assassinate.*
- Be aware of the emotive connotations in certain words: 'the popular singer *confessed* that she was married' has a different sense from 'the popular singer *stated* that she was married'. Why?
- Consider the effects of choosing different verbs to describe actions. The following piece of writing contains some very neutral verbs:

The teacher came into the room. She sat down on her chair and spoke to the class. They listened to what she said and then did the work she gave them. At the end of the lesson the teacher dismissed the class. They left the room.

This can be made into a more interesting piece of writing by changing the verbs used and adding adverbs to clarify their meaning, for example:

The teacher strode briskly into the room. She perched fiercely on her chair and sternly addressed the class. They paid close attention to what she instructed them to do and then fearfully attempted the work which she had dictated to them. At the end of the lesson the teacher ordered the class to dismiss. They crept silently from the room.

The writer of this version has deliberately chosen words to create a rather negative and unwelcoming atmosphere in the classroom.

● **Try this** Rewrite the original paragraph above by using different verbs, adverbs and adjectives to create a more pleasant and welcoming atmosphere.

Adjectives, similes and metaphors

- All of these are valuable tools in producing good writing. However, they should not be overused. Always try to think of original expressions which help to give your reader a clear picture and try to avoid tired and unhelpful expressions. 'He ran like the wind' does not really give a clear picture to the reader, but 'He ran like an antelope fleeing from a pack of lions' is more original and allows the writer to suggest fear and desperation in the character's actions.
- Long lists of adjectives and a simile attached to every noun have the effect of slowing down your writing and taking away much of its dynamism. Be selective.

Making accurate and effective use of grammatical structures, sentences, punctuation and spelling

Accuracy

- The examiners will be looking for evidence that you can use punctuation correctly. They will expect you to be in control of full stops in particular. The most serious punctuation error made by IGCSE students is to use a comma to separate sentences when you should use a full stop.
- Other punctuation marks which you will be expected to use confidently within sentences are commas and apostrophes. These basic skills should be shown by students aiming for a grade C.
- However, there are other punctuation devices whose correct use will be seen as a positive merit by examiners. These include semi-colons, colons, dashes and speech marks. If you are able to use these accurately and confidently then your writing is likely to be of the sophisticated quality required to achieve top grades.

Sentences

The sentence is the basic unit of English expression. Good writing consists of a range of appropriately used sentence types and the ability to demonstrate that you can do this will result in high marks for the writing tasks. The main types of sentences are:

- **Simple**: short sentences containing only one main statement. For example: *The girls were eating their lunch.*
- **Compound**: sentences in which two or more statements are joined together by the use of conjunctions. For example: *The girls were eating their lunch and the boys were playing football.*
- **Complex**: sentences in which one main statement (or clause) is developed by subordinate clauses and phrases which expand on the main point being made. They can be quite short, for example: *When I leave here, I am going home* or quite long: *While the girls were eating their lunch, the boys, who were playing football on the field behind the dining-room which had its windows open because of the heat, were making so much noise that the girls had difficulty hearing what each other was saying.*

Obviously, complex sentences can carry a much wider range of linked ideas than simple sentences and are able to convey more sophisticated and complicated ideas. Examiners will reward students who show control of complex sentences, so it is important to be confident in using them.

Examiner's tips

▶ *How* you express yourself is just as important as *what* you say. Don't over-complicate the content of your writing.

▶ The examiner is a complete stranger who may live far away from you. Keep this in your mind as you write. (S)he is unlikely to have any knowledge of the area in which you live. If you are describing something in your locality it is important that you include some basic scene-setting details.

▶ The examiner will not be familiar with the colloquial language you use with your friends. Different countries have different dialect words for the same thing which may not be universally known. This is why it is important to write your essays in standard English.

▶ The examiner wants to be interested and entertained by your work. (S)he would like to get to know a little bit about you and your surroundings. Think of your reader as someone you are meeting for the first time and on whom you want to make a good impression. Do this by making yourself interesting and by being polite. Don't present a false image of yourself – it's hard work to keep up the pretence.

▶ Don't try to use over-elaborate language but make sure that you choose your words carefully and express them in accurately punctuated sentences. Examiners expect you to use correct punctuation; confusion will arise if you fail to do so.

▶ Examiners do not like to be confused; the more they have to stop and try to work out what you mean, the more confusing they will find what you have written.

▶ Keep what you have written focused on the task.

▶ Pay careful attention to the type of writing you are doing. For example, don't take a narrative approach to a title that requires you to write to inform.

▶ If you are asked to write within a specific genre (a letter, a magazine article, etc.) use language and a register that are appropriate to that genre.

▶ Good writing uses a range of devices which are suitable to the writer's purpose and so a variety of sentence structures is necessary to keep your readers interested. A short, sharp sentence can be used very effectively in the middle of complex sentences by a writer who is in control of what (s)he is doing.

TOPIC 7 Argumentative writing

Key objectives
- To make sure that you understand what argumentative writing is
- To help you to understand the way that argumentative writing is marked by examiners
- To make sure that you understand the common mistakes that students make when tackling argumentative writing tasks
- To consider strategies for approaching argumentative writing tasks

Key definitions

Term	Definition
Argumentative	Argumentative tasks may require you to write in order to argue, persuade or advise or for a combination of these purposes. You will be expected to pay particular attention to the structure and organisation of your ideas and to write in a logical and balanced register, in general by using formal vocabulary
Argue	To write a logically structured and developed sequence of ideas to justify or oppose a point of view. You should adopt an objective tone and vocabulary
Persuade	To encourage your readers to agree with your point of view. You might want to use some emotive language and examples to encourage them to do so
Advise	You are telling your reader(s) about something of which you have experience and are trying to make them appreciate its value for them. You are likely to be addressing your reader(s) directly and semi-formally

Key ideas
- Argumentative writing is where the examiner is asking you *to put forward and to justify your views* for or against a particular point of view or proposal.
- Your writing should be carefully planned.
- You should support your opinions with facts or examples wherever possible.
- A clear introduction and a forceful conclusion will help to convince the examiner to agree with your ideas.
- If you are given a specific audience for your writing, use vocabulary and a register that are appropriate to it.

Common misconceptions and errors

Argumentative writing means that you have to quarrel with the wording of the title. Wrong! ▪

Argumentative writing requires you to write a story. Wrong! ▪

Sample question and answers

Sample question 'The planet Earth is doomed!' What do you think?

Planning your work

- There are clues in the question as to how to tackle it.

- Focus your answer by asking yourself questions, such as:
  - Why should anyone think the Earth is doomed?
  - How far is it true?
  - What sort of things could be destroying the planet?
  - Who is to blame?
  - What evidence have I got that this statement is true?

*An exclamation mark suggests that
the statement is open to question*

'The planet Earth is doomed!' What do you think?

You are asked what you think

  - Is there anything that can be done?

  These questions will provide your topic sentences.

- Before you start to write, decide on the *stance* your argument will take:
  - Are you going to agree fully with the statement?
  - Are you going to disagree completely with it?
  - Or will you consider reasons for thinking it could be true, reasons for thinking that it is not true and try to reach a balanced conclusion?

- Examiners will not have any 'right' or 'wrong' answers in their minds but they will expect you to produce a logically structured argument.

Student's answer Weapons of mass destruction; the disappearance of the ozone layer; global warming; killer epidemics such as AIDS and SARS; collision with a giant asteroid are all very good reasons for thinking this statement might be true. Certainly the world's media delight in presenting scenarios of doom and gloom and it is indeed within the capabilities of human beings to destroy the Earth if they decide to make a concerted effort to do so. However, although these threats to our lives are serious issues of concern, the fact remains that we are concerned about them and a large number of the inhabitants of the globe on which we live are prepared to do something about them. It is exciting and tempting to take a sensationalist approach to this topic but perhaps it would be better and more productive to stop and consider rationally how likely it is that the prophets of doom are right in their predictions.

Examiner's comments   *This is a forceful and effective opening paragraph. The student has confronted us with some topics which (s)he will be able to deal with in the rest of the essay. The opening sentence immediately grabs the reader's attention and this allows the writer to be confident that (s)he has the reader's engagement, so that (s)he can present a personal point of view more directly towards the end of the paragraph. The student has clearly signalled the direction which the argument will take; (s)he is aware of the arguments for thinking the Earth is doomed but is going to present us with counter-arguments as to why we should take the threat seriously but not capitulate to it. This opening paragraph provides plenty of opportunity for further development.*

The tone of this student's writing is fully appropriate to the task; (s)he uses a formal register with very well controlled complex sentences but, nevertheless, succeeds in addressing the readers directly and in a way that fully involves them through the writer's clear emotional engagement with the argument (s)he is presenting. The spelling is correct throughout; the vocabulary is precise and it is worth noting that (s)he exhibits confident and secure understanding of when to use the semi-colon.

Student's answer   I suppose the Earth could be doomed, especially if we get invaded by aliens from outer space, they could have been watching us for a long time and want to take over the Earth for there own perposes. On the other hand people on Earth mite destroy themselves as we keep poluting our planet with different things and you couldn't do very much about stopping them now that it's so much all over the place.

Examiner's comments   *This is not a focused opening. The student begins with an idea which (s)he cannot sustain and which is not very convincing. (S)he does not develop the point about alien invasions and then suddenly introduces the idea of man-made pollution destroying the planet. (S)he has not expressed her/himself very clearly in the final sentence (perhaps not thinking through the ideas carefully before starting to write) and the reader is confused by what (s)he is trying to say. This is not an effective opening paragraph as it does not provide a clear introduction or direction to the essay and does not allow the writer the opportunity to develop and structure her/his ideas. It also tries to cram together two separate points which would better have been the topics of two distinct paragraphs.*

The tone of this student's writing is colloquial without any clear indication of the audience at which it is aimed, nor does it immediately engage the reader. There are several spelling errors of simple vocabulary and a serious error of sentence separation. The vocabulary also lacks precision and interest. These limitations result in communication being blurred and the reader not having a clear understanding of what the writer is trying to say.

● **Try this**   Using the first student's opening paragraph as a starting point, make your own plan of how the essay would continue. Write out the plan, paragraph by paragraph, using the following suggestions as a guide:

<u>Reasons for thinking the Earth is doomed</u>
(*You could use the ideas in the student's opening paragraph but each one needs to be developed.*)

Reasons for thinking the Earth is not doomed

(*Again, you could develop the student's ideas.*)

Conclusion

(*Sum up the points already made and refer back to the question.*)

Now that you've planned your ideas, write your essay in full.

> **Examiner's tip**
> ▶ The plan will have given you some ideas but think about how you will organise them. Is it better to deal with points for and against each idea or do you want to deal first with all the points for and then all the points against? It doesn't matter which approach you take but it's a good idea to decide before you start to write.

Sample question What do you think are the best ways of keeping order in school?

Planning your work

- You could start by identifying the key words in the sentence and then considering them closely. For example:

Key words	What does this mean?
What do you think?	The question is asking for *your* opinion. Try to base your comments on your own experience. You are asked to say what you think, so the examiners will not be looking for any 'right' or 'wrong' ideas but will want a well-structured argument backed up by examples
the best ways	Are these ways which are best for the teachers, the students or both? It's up to you to decide. Should you consider the ways teachers impose order or the ways students keep themselves in control?
keeping order	Does this phrase refer to order during lessons or order throughout the school in general? You'll probably want to consider both situations but you might want to make different suggestions for each. Could the phrase simply mean keeping records?
in school	Are you going to base your comments here specifically on your experiences in the schools you've attended or are you going to make more general philosophical points about all schools? Probably the best approach is to write about your own experiences first and then apply some more general conclusions

- Simply by looking closely at the wording of the question, you can make quite a lot of points and provide yourself with a good basis for a plan. In an examination, however, you must be careful to keep the time restrictions in mind. Don't plan to produce something which is over-ambitious in length.

● **Try this** Here are some more example argumentative topics; practise planning and writing some of them and then use the answer guide on **pages 73–75** to assess your response.

1 'There are boys' subjects and there are girls' subjects; what's the point in mixing them up?' How far do you agree with this comment on the school curriculum?

2 'Travel broadens the mind.' How would you set about persuading someone to agree with this view?

3 Is there any cause to be concerned about the rapid advance of technology?

4 'The behaviour of professional sportsmen and women is not a good example to the younger generation.' Write a speech in which you try to persuade your fellow students to agree or disagree with this statement.

Examiner's tips

▶ Argumentative writing tasks often appear to be very far-reaching: don't fall into the trap of trying to cover too many major issues in your answer. Plan carefully.

▶ You need not include more than four or five main points as long as they are developed in detail.

▶ Try not to include too many generalised statements; illustrate all of your main points with specific details and examples.

▶ Use vocabulary and a register appropriate to your audience but don't forget that your *real* audience is the examiner.

▶ If you are writing a speech, try to make it sound authentic by using phrases that are directed at your imagined listeners, but don't write in such a colloquial way that the examiner is unable to understand clearly what you mean.

▶ Argumentative writing is difficult, especially under examination conditions, so remember that you have a choice of topics; you don't have to choose the argumentative option.

▶ If you enjoy this type of writing then it's a good idea to make some preparations. Read newspapers and magazines so that you have an understanding of key issues and some examples which you can use to support your arguments.

▶ When you read what people have to say about a particular issue, practise thinking of opposing arguments to those they are putting forward.

▶ Always try to see both sides of an argument; good argumentative writing is controlled by the mind; you must control your feelings and express them as a logical argument.

TOPIC 8 Discursive writing

Key objectives

- To make sure that you understand what discursive writing is
- To help you to understand the way that discursive writing is marked by examiners
- To make sure that you understand the common mistakes that students make when tackling discursive writing tasks
- To consider strategies for approaching discursive writing tasks

Key definitions

Term	Definition
Discursive	Discursive tasks may require you to write in order to analyse, review or comment or for a combination of these purposes. You will be expected to organise your ideas as you think best and to adopt a reflective approach rather than a tightly structured series of arguments. You are able to choose your audience and can adopt a variety of approaches. For example, you could adopt an analytical approach, in which case you would use a formal register, or a more personal, informal exploration of the different implications the topic has for you
Analyse	To break down something into its component parts. When you are writing in order to analyse something, you will be making an objective consideration of the different issues with which the topic is concerned
Review	To write an overall survey of a subject or a general criticism of it. In other words, you are considering its qualities (strengths and weaknesses) and coming to a balanced conclusion about them
Comment	To give your own point of view on a topic. However, you should try to present balanced statements rather than purely emotional ones

Key ideas

- Discursive writing tasks allow you considerable freedom of interpretation and approach. It is important that you give yourself a clear *focus* in order to be consistent in what you write.
- Make your writing sound relaxed and natural; in order to do this you need to spend some time thinking about and planning what you are going to write.
- Don't get too carried away and try to include more material than you have time to deal with.
- You don't have to adopt a strictly chronological approach when producing a piece of discursive writing but each point in your essay should be seen to relate to the central topic.
- This type of task allows you to express your own personality and individuality; you can impress examiners with how you express yourself as much as by what you say.

Sample questions and answers

Sample question 1 'Choice'

> **Examiner's tip**
> ▶ Like many discursive writing tasks, this is a one-word title; it provides you with a lot of opportunities but you need to define your approach so that the reader is aware of the course your writing will take.

Planning your work

There are many ways of producing plans for writing tasks; with a topic such as 'Choice' a spider diagram might be the best approach. For example:

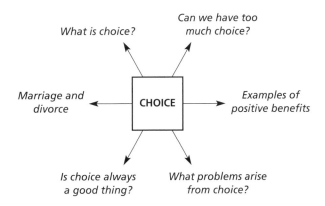

Student's answer

Examiner's comments	Essay
This is a good positive opening statement which clearly sets out the writer's opinion.	'Choice' is a wonderful thing in my opinion.
A good opening paragraph which clearly allows scope for development and focuses directly on the topic. Accurately expressed, too, apart from a missing comma after 'However'.	It gives us the freedom to live our lives to the full, and if we make a wrong choice, we can learn from our mistakes. However some people would argue that too much choice could be harmful to us and I agree that certain circumstances can mean choice can cause many problems.
The student is aware of the need to vary the vocabulary to maintain the reader's interest; (s)he's using 'options' instead of 'choices'.	A large variety of options means that when choosing one, a lot of consideration and thinking has to be done about each one.
This clearly links back to and expands on the point made in the opening paragraph; this is a good, cohesive piece of writing so far (apart from the missing comma after 'however').	However this can lead to more confusion. As you find out more information about a choice, this can lead you to like the option more and more. If this is the case in several options, we can find it impossible to come to a decision and our minds can be thrown into turmoil about what to do.

continued

Examiner's comments	Essay
Again, this statement will allow development into the next paragraph. Expression is still accurate with a variety of sentence structures.	In such scenarios as these, choice is seen as a negative thing.
This is a clear development of the idea of choice as a negative thing; the point about pressure resulting from too many decisions could perhaps be expanded in more detail and the essay is beginning to rely a bit too much on generalised statements. Expression is still good, although (s)he's confused 'affected' and 'effected'.	In more serious cases, too much choice can lead to anxiety, depression and suicide. With many important decisions to make in our lives, fear of making the wrong one can lead our eyes to be blinded to what we really want. With such high levels of confusion and pressure to make the correct choice inside us, our emotions can be seriously effected and can become very complex and therefore negative.
Good! (S)he's introducing a concrete example to reinforce the general points (s)he's been making earlier.	Another example of choice as a negative thing can be seen in marriages.
Good use of statistics to support a point of view.	Divorce rates are now extremely high, with one in three marriages ending in divorce in some Western countries.
This is a well developed point and it's staying focused on the title.	This is mainly because the option of divorce is always there and is easy to choose. With divorces being so easy to obtain, it is easy to see why many marriages end in divorce at the first sign of trouble. This means many people lose their partners and many children lose the strong family unit they once had. Divorce is only as common as it is, because it is an easy choice to choose.
This is still dealing with the negative aspects of choice. There's perhaps an attempt to include too much in this paragraph and it might have been better to develop these ideas over two paragraphs rather than one; however, this is done under examination conditions and time is limited.	If there were laws to ban divorce, couples would find a solution to their problems because they had to, and as a result many marriages would be saved. All these points illustrate that although many people view choice as a positive thing, there is a more sinister side to it. Choice can be negative resulting in hurt, depression and high levels of confusion. In some rare cases choice can prove to be very dangerous to your health and wellbeing.
This is a very good sentence to introduce a concluding paragraph and to link it in with everything that has gone before.	Despite all of these points, I believe that overall choice is a gift.
Expression is a little insecure here, as there's a confusion of number between noun and pronoun.	It allows us to be an individual and live our lives to the full in the way we want to.
A comma, at last!	'You've never had it so good' is a phrase that describes how choice can create a life which is free and with a large diversity of experiences. However, I can

This is a thorough, thoughtful and well constructed response to the task. The student is aware of the time constraints and has not tried to write too much. (S)he's sensibly concentrated on only one main aspect of 'Choice' and developed the comments fully. There's a very clear grasp of the topic; the expression is mainly accurate; spelling is good and register and vocabulary are fully appropriate to the topic and approach. The conclusion is a little hurried, but that's fully understandable considering the time restraints. This is a Band 1 piece of writing.

understand that too much choice can bring many problems. I think in the end, it depends on the individual and on what type of person you are.

Student's answer Many people believe that we have too many choices in life and that problems are caused by the choices we choose to make in our lives.

Some people would argue that having alot of choice is good. We are offered lots of paths to take in our lives and we are able to choose our options, careers, entertainment etc. These people think this is a good thing because its a chance to show our individuality and the way people lead their lives in very different ways.

Other people would disagree and say that too much choice is bad and causes lots of problems. Experts believe anxiety, depression and suicide are at record levels because we are faced with too many choices. Religious people could also believe too much choice is bad and that divorce shouldn't be an option in marriage as it should be forever.

I think that having alot of choice in different things is a good thing. The choices we make show who we are as individuals and choices are what make us different. If we had no choice in things then I think that would cause more problems than having too many. Everyone would be doing the same thing, the same way. There would be no differences. Choices can sometimes be stressful but I think life would be dull without them.

● **Try this** Although the second student's essay uses many similar points to those made by the first student, it was assessed as being no better than a Band 3 piece of writing. Can you think why this should be?

Copy the table on page 62 and make your own comments on different aspects of what this student has written. Then refer to the writing answer guide on **pages 73–75** to see how this confirms the band awarded. Remember to note both good and bad points and then decide which mark-band criteria best fit the piece of writing.

Feature	Comment
Vocabulary/register	
Content	
Accuracy of expression	
Accuracy of spelling	
Accuracy of punctuation	
Development and linking of ideas	

Sample question 2   What makes a 'special friend'?

Planning your work

How would you set about planning for this? One way to get your ideas in order is to ask yourself some fairly straightforward questions which will help you to focus on the task. You'll find that each question very soon leads on to another and so you will be able to put your ideas into some sort of sequence. Here are some questions you could ask yourself:

- Which friend should I choose?
- What makes this friend special?
- What does the word 'special' mean here?
- Do I have to write about a real friend or can it be an imaginary one?
- How much detail should I give when I describe the friend?
- Would it be best to concentrate on the qualities that make a friend special, rather than just describing someone?
- Perhaps I could write about a special friend who comprises the best qualities of lots of different people I know.

- Should I include an account of an incident or incidents in which the friend's qualities were especially important?
- If so, which incident or incidents?
- How am I going to start writing on this topic? Should I start by describing the friend?
- Should I start with a question such as 'What is a special friend'?

● **Try this**

1 What other questions can you think of relating to a 'special friend'? Add some more to the list above and then look back over them.
- Which are the most important ones?
- Which of the others link most readily with these?
- Which should be discarded for the purpose of this particular essay?
Of those above, the final question provides you with a good starting point but it arises as a result of some of the others.

2 Here are some more example discursive topics; practise planning and writing some of them and then use the answer guide on **pages 73–75** to assess your response.
a) Vegetarianism
b) Likes and dislikes
c) Baby-sitting
d) Reasons to be cheerful

Examiner's tips

▶ Discursive writing tasks are very open-ended: it is important that you impose you own limitations on your response.
▶ It is unlikely that you will be given an audience for your writing; decide on your audience before you start to write.
▶ Discursive writing tasks require you to explore different areas relating to one central issue. Make sure that you don't fall into the trap of writing a narrative story.
▶ You do not have to adopt too formal a tone when writing discursively.
▶ If the task allows, it is a good idea to write in the first person and refer to personal experience and what you have learned from it.
▶ Make yourself and your thoughts interesting; examiners enjoy the experience of making the acquaintance of interesting personalities through reading what they have to write.
▶ You can make yourself interesting through how you write as well as what you write about.

TOPIC 9 Descriptive writing

Key objectives

- To make sure that you understand what descriptive writing is
- To help you to understand the way that descriptive writing is marked by examiners
- To make sure that you understand the common mistakes that students make when tackling descriptive writing tasks
- To consider strategies for approaching descriptive writing tasks

Key definitions

Term	Definition
Descriptive writing	Descriptive writing tasks may require you to describe, inform or explain. It is important that you have a clear picture in your own mind of what you are describing before you start to write and that you carefully choose vocabulary, similes, and so on to convey as complete a picture as you can to your readers. There are two main types of descriptive writing. You may be asked to give a factual description of something, in which case your main focus will be to inform or explain and you should use vocabulary and a register appropriate to this. More likely with IGCSE First Language English, you will be asked to write a more imaginative type of description. This requires you to use language in an imaginative way in order to recreate in the mind of the reader the impression of what you are describing
Inform	To provide your audience with facts and details about something. Information is something that can be checked and verified and informative writing does not require you to give your opinion on the issue involved
Explain	To illustrate the meaning of something in order to make it clearly understood by the reader. It may be necessary to adapt your vocabulary and register in order to make your explanation clear to your readers
Describe	To give an account of something or to produce a picture in words. IGCSE descriptive essay titles are likely to ask you to describe a place or person

Key ideas

- When writing a description it is best to think of an actual place or person well known to you as a basis for your writing; you can always add extra details to the description to make your writing more interesting.
- Try to see things from the perspective of your reader. It is very easy to assume that the reader knows everything you do about what you are describing. However, failure to include what to you is an obvious detail may cause considerable confusion for someone else.
- Don't confuse the different types of descriptive writing; a poetic, imaginative style is not suitable for a purely informative task.

- Choose your words carefully to give as detailed and precise a description as possible. Adjectives, similes and metaphors are all valuable descriptive devices but don't forget the importance of well-chosen verbs and adverbs.

Sample questions and answers

Sample questions 1 Describe a sport or game which you enjoy playing or watching and explain why.

2 Describe a place you know well as it appears at two different times.

Examiner's tips

▶ Question 1 requires a factual description of the sport, not an account of your finest achievements! However, you may be able to refer to those when you explain why you enjoy it.

▶ Question 2 requires an imaginative use of language; don't just try to describe how the place looks, but think of sounds and smells associated with it as well. Think about contrast here.

Planning your work for Question 1

- Look at the key words in the question. It gives you some choices; make use of them to focus your ideas.
- Whether you choose a sport or a game and whether it is something you enjoy playing or watching is up to you, but write about something with which you are familiar.
- Once you've decided, you must think of what you will include in your description of it – don't get too technical – and also reasons why you enjoy it.
- If you choose a favourite computer game, the examiner may never have heard of it; you'll need to give some basic information so that (s)he is aware of what it involves.
- By now, the structure of what you are going to write is becoming clear; here is a skeleton plan:
  - *Paragraph 1* Introduce the sport/game. Explain what it involves; the number of players; where and when it's played
  - *Paragraph 2* More particular details of the sport/game, perhaps with some examples of tactics and descriptions of some actual incidents which you have witnessed or been involved in
  - *Paragraphs 3 and 4* Why you find the activity so enjoyable; include both general reasons and personal accounts to explain and illustrate your points
  - *Paragraph 5* Conclusion; sum up the points you've made about the sport/game and why you enjoy it and then try to involve the reader in your conclusion, perhaps by suggesting reasons why other people (even examiners) might also enjoy the activity.

● **Try this** Here are some topic sentences which follow on from the skeleton plan above; use them as a guide for your own essay on this topic. Try to write using the same register as the topic sentences. You should aim to write about 80–100 words for each paragraph.

1 _____ is a sport/game which I very much enjoy; it is played by many people around the world and involves …
(*You can decide what the sport or game will be and should give details of how many players, teams are involved in it.*)

2 However, the more skilled you become at the sport/game, the more interesting and entertaining it becomes. For example, …
(*At this stage you can start to describe some of the more complicated tactics involved in the activity you have chosen.*)

3 As you can see, there are many interesting features about this sport/game and the ones which I find most enjoyable are …
(*This is where you can start to describe your enjoyment of the activity, but don't forget to say* why *you find it enjoyable.*)

4 I remember at least two exciting and rewarding moments which happened when I was involved in playing/watching _____.
(*Now you can describe some actual incidents in which you were involved but do link them to your explanation of why you find the activity enjoyable.*)

5 Now I've told you all about _____ and why I enjoy it so much; I think everybody should try this activity because …
(*Finish off by summing up what you've already said and then adding one or two points which you've deliberately kept to the end so that you can finish on a positive and forceful note.*)

Planning your work for Question 2

- First, think of the place you are going to describe. It should be somewhere you know – don't over-complicate matters by trying to make up a place, it's not that sort of task.
- The place may be in the town or the country, it may be somewhere well known or just known to you. However, don't assume that the examiner will know it; you must give some background details.
- You've been asked to describe the place at two different times; this instruction has deliberately been left vague – it's up to you whether you want to describe two different times of the day/week/month/year.
- However, it's important that you describe contrasting times and use language that reinforces your description.
- There should be no problems with structuring your description, but try to link the two sections of it to show that you have a good overview of the scene.

Student's answer Movement is a serious danger; wherever you go you are at risk, either from the preoccupied busy office worker striding along, swinging his hard briefcase with no thought for who might be in its path or from young boys, late for school, weaving in and out of pedestrians as they ride their bicycles along the pavement. The main road is one long snake of vehicles, writhing along at frightening speed. There is no break in its length and the opposite pavement might as well be the other side of the world for all the hope there is of reaching it. The doors of shops continually open and close as customers squeeze in and out; their interiors are full of harassed shop assistants and fraught customers. Everyone is shouting as the metallic, grinding wail of the traffic makes ordinary conversation impossible. This is every morning in the city. …

In the evening, the city centre is quiet as the shopkeepers and business people have left and there are only a few individuals walking around, talking to their friends. The cafés and restaurants are beginning to prepare for the invasion of the night's customers and as the day light fades, their welcoming interior lights spill out on to the pavements, creating little circles of warmth. The air is filled with the pungent aromas of garlic and other cooking ingredients and where earlier there had been swarms of cars snarling along the streets, there are now flocks of small birds, alighting in the town square, feeding off the discarded food left by the daytime visitors and filling the surroundings with their gentle twitterings.

Examiner's comments

The student has produced two effectively contrasting descriptions. The scenes have been clearly visualised and (s)he has sensibly chosen to focus on only limited areas and describe them in some detail. Especially pleasing is the way (s)he has varied the sentence structures to create particular effects. The passage describing the early morning begins with a positive, almost threatening statement and the sentence structures throughout the paragraph reflect the frenzied activity that is being described. However, the rhythms of the sentences in the second paragraph are much gentler and convey the quiet and peace of the evening.

The student has used descriptive language such as metaphors well (although the comparison of the traffic with a snake is perhaps a little strained). (S)he has chosen words carefully, in particular the adjectives and verbs, and the reader is left with a clear understanding of what it is like to be in this city at the times of day (s)he is describing. This is clearly a Band 1 piece of writing.

● Try this

Here are some more example descriptive writing tasks. (It may be a good idea to work with a friend so that you can read through each other's work and make constructive criticisms.)

1 Describe how you think *your* life will change during the next twenty years.
2 Describe the most beautiful place you have ever visited, explaining your feelings for it.
3 Write a letter to a cousin who will shortly be starting at your school, informing them about the school curriculum and explaining what to do on her/his first day there.
4 Write a description of a person who is considered to be eccentric.

Examiner's tips

▶ Descriptive writing tasks can be very general: it is important that you base your description on someone or something within your own experience so that you have a clear picture in your mind of what you intend to describe.

▶ Suit your vocabulary and register to the type of task you are answering. Writing to *inform* requires a more objective/impersonal tone than writing to *describe*.

▶ Stay clearly focused on the task. Description is not the same as persuasion!

▶ Your reader is unlikely to have any knowledge of what you are describing so a clear introduction to your writing is important. Don't assume that the reader will have any awareness of what may seem obvious to you.

▶ Try to use similes and metaphors that are interesting and original. It is very easy to fall back on clichés when you are writing descriptively; avoid them!

▶ Don't overuse adjectives as too many can slow down the pace of your writing. Try to use interesting verbs and adverbs to communicate a clear picture of who or what you are describing.

TOPIC 10 Narrative writing

Key objectives

- To make sure that you understand what narrative writing is
- To help you to understand the way that narrative writing is marked by examiners
- To make sure that you understand the common mistakes that students make when tackling narrative writing tasks
- To consider strategies for approaching narrative writing tasks

Key definitions

Term	Definition
Narrative writing	Narrative tasks may require you to write a story or part of a story; they may also ask you to write a true account. The purpose of your writing is to entertain the reader through the situation you have imagined and also to explore that situation and the characters involved in it
True account	A narrative description of something that actually happened. However, an examiner is not going to worry whether your account is completely true or not. It should be made sufficiently convincing to appear to be true
Entertain	A piece of writing that entertains and involves the readers and gives them some pleasure or enjoyment as they read it. You need not try to be amusing or comic in order to entertain; a well constructed and planned story with carefully chosen vocabulary will be sufficient
Imagine	Something imagined is something original that you have created within your own mind. However, you will be assessed primarily on your writing skills, not on the quality of your imagination. Make sure that what you write about is convincing
Explore	When you are writing to explore, you are attempting to develop the implications of an imagined situation as fully as you can within the time available to you

Examiner's tips

▶ Remember how much time you have in the exam.
▶ Don't try to write too complicated a story. Examiners want quality not quantity.
▶ Don't fill your writing with direct speech; it causes problems with punctuation and it's difficult to use effectively. Just use a little to show that you are in control of it.
▶ Writing a story is not just about narrative; description of characters and setting is as important.
▶ It may help you to base your story on something that has (or might have) happened to you. You can then embroider the situation as seems best.
▶ Don't take a story you may have read (or written) before and try to make it fit the title on the question paper – examiners will be able to see the joins!
▶ Don't forget to use paragraphs.

Key Ideas

- Planning what you are going to write is crucial; the opening sentence allows you the opportunity to develop a story in many different directions. Think about what direction you will take – and where it will end – before you start to write.

- For example, the sample question below could be the start of a mystery story. What will you find behind the closed door? Or you could write about a more everyday experience. Perhaps the corridor is in a school, the closed door is that of the Headteacher's study, and you have been summoned there.

- Wherever you decide to set a story, you must make it convincing to the reader by including background details. For example, at what time of the day (or night) is the story going to start? Who else, apart from the central character, is going to be involved? How much detail or description will you give of the characters involved in the story? For example, in the sample question below how much time will you spend in describing the corridor, the walk to the door and what is to be found behind it?

- Are you going to write your story in the first or third person? It's your choice, but a first person narrative will be centred on the experiences of the narrator; a third person narrative will allow a wider viewpoint but may lead to an over-complex account.

- Make sure that your continuation is consistent with the tense used in the opening sentence. As an example, the opening sentence of the sample question below is written in the past continuous tense; the rest of the story should continue in the same tense.

Sample question and answers

Sample question   Write a story that starts with these words: 'At the end of the corridor, the closed door was waiting.'

Student's answer   At the end of the corridor, the closed door was waiting. The clock that sat in the middle of the narrow passageway counted down the minutes, before the interrigation would begin.

'Heena Patel!' came a cold voice from behind the Headmaster's office door. Heena stood up, leaving only Sally in the corridor. She dragged her guilty feet along the freshly varnished floor of the menacing corridor. She turned to see Sally hiding behind the long blonde hair that covered her face. Just for a second, Heena caught a glimpse of her face, as a grey tear camouflaged itself in the miserable expression that now enhabited her face.

There were no lights in the corridor and as the afternoon became evening, a casting shadow gradually made its way the length of the corridor. Sally sat slouched, terrified that Mr Shah, the Headmaster, would find out their terrible deed.

Examiner's comments   *This student has tried hard to create a threatening atmosphere through both the details and the vocabulary (s)he has chosen. Words such as* narrow, interrogation, menacing *and* camouflaged *all suggest a sense of fear and a feeling of something wrong which is being kept hidden. This is reinforced by the fact that it is getting dark and that evening is casting a* *shadow over the scene. The student has chosen to describe the events by using a third person narrative and has set the story in surroundings with which (s)he is familiar. (S)he has introduced two further characters, Sally and the Headmaster, and has given sufficient details about them for the reader to have an impression of what their characters are like and what part they are going to play in the story. (S)he has created a convincing scenario and provided a clear direction in which the story can develop. There are a few spelling mistakes but they don't impair understanding.*

Student's answer

At the end of the corridor, the closed door was waiting. I tried to focus on it, but every time I did my mind was distracted by the misty atmosphere. We couldn't turn back now. Not after coming this far. Our destiny was now within arms reach but something felt strange, not right.

'Are you sure about this?' asked Harry.

'No,' I replied, 'but it must be done anyway.'

I looked at Harry; he seemed nervous and lost. But come to think of it, I was too.

As we inched closer to the huge, dark door I felt adrenaline pumping around my body and although nothing felt normal, Harry and myself kept on walking slowly, step by step.

'We can turn back now,' whispered Harry.

I tried to ignore him. I didn't speak, because I knew if we walked through that door, our lives would never be the same again.

Examiner's comments

This student has taken a different approach from the other, but an equally successful one. (S)he is writing in the first person and is concentrating very much on the state of mind of the narrator and the one other character in the story. (S)he has deliberately not revealed full details of the surroundings or the situation in order to create an atmosphere of suspense. This has been added to by the use of short, taut sentences and the effective inclusion of direct speech. The pronoun 'it' is repeatedly used to refer to the deed which is to be done, and this is another effective way of involving the readers in the narrative as it implies that we are already part of the events. The final sentence of the extract prepares the readers to expect that something significant is about to happen and allows the writer the opportunity to move on to the next stage of the story.

● Try this

Write your own continuation of one or both of the stories above. Before you start to write, think carefully about how you will structure your narrative. The following general questions and suggestions might help you:

- How will you conclude your story? Should you finish with a clear-cut resolution which ties up all the issues or should you leave your readers in mid-air, wondering what will happen next?
- How will you develop the characters already introduced? Do you want to add some unexpected details about them or have the readers been given sufficient information already?
- How many more episodes should you include? What will they be?

- As you have limited time under examination conditions, don't plan to include too many twists and turns in your story but allow room in your plan to develop the details of each episode sufficiently to make it interesting and convincing.
- Continue using the same tone and register as the opening of the story.

Here are some suggestions as to how each story could be continued – you don't have to use them if you can think of other ideas.

Story 1

- Decide why Heena and Sally are in trouble. Perhaps they've been accused of theft or bullying. Are they guilty? Were they both involved in the episode? You don't have to give away the ending at this point but you must decide what it will be.
- You could continue by following Heena into the Headmaster's office and describing the interview. What is the Headmaster's attitude to Heena? What are her thoughts and feelings as she listens to what he has to say? What is she accused of? How does she answer his questions? There's a good opportunity here to show that you can handle direct speech.
- You could prolong the suspense of your story by switching back to describe what Sally is thinking as she waits outside and can see the silhouettes of Heena and the Headmaster through the door, but can't hear what is being said.
- Perhaps Sally is guilty of the crime and Heena is being bullied by her to take the blame. You could conclude the story by describing how the Headmaster discovers the truth and what happens to Sally.

Story 2

- First decide whether or not you intend to reveal at any point what is behind the door. Be careful not to produce something that is too much of an anti-climax.
- The opening of the story suggests that there's something mysterious involved, perhaps a ghost story, but be careful – concentrate on building atmosphere and suspense and don't give away too much yet.
- You could continue by developing the relationship between the narrator and Harry and explain why they are there. Perhaps you could include a flashback describing the events leading up to this moment.
- Next you could continue describing what happens as the characters approach the door. Concentrate on building up the atmosphere of suspense and fear. What are their thoughts and feelings? You could develop Harry's fears.
- Your final paragraph could focus on the opening of the door; it's your decision whether or not you describe what is behind it. One way of ending the story might be to write a paragraph set several years in the future as the narrator looks back to the episode described in the rest of the story and recounts her/his feelings. As you're writing in the first person, it's likely that the narrator survived the experience!

● **Try this** At the top of the next page are some more example narrative writing tasks. Plan your ideas carefully before you start to write and in particular concentrate on describing the setting and characters in order to produce a convincing background in which to set your story.

1 Write a story which starts with these words: 'It was too hot and I couldn't concentrate on the work that my father had given me to do.'

2 'The Tree.' Write a story with this title.

3 'The Day I Broke the Rules.' Write a story or a true account with this title.

4 Write a story in which a misunderstanding between two people results in an unexpected outcome.

Examiner's tips

▶ Narrative writing tasks can appear attractive, but when you're writing under examination conditions make sure that you can restrict the content of your story to the time available; it's easy to get carried away.

▶ Keep your readers in mind at all times; structure your story in such a way that you keep them involved.

▶ Try to keep what you write within your own experience; stories about alien abductions or special agent adventures written by students do not usually convince adult readers.

▶ Try to avoid cliché situations, especially concluding your story with the words 'and then I woke up to find it was all a dream'!

▶ Make sure that your story is written consistently in the same tense; it is usually more effective to write in the past rather than the present tense.

How continuous writing tasks are marked

All the different types of continuous writing described will be marked out of a total of 25. This comprises two different marks: a maximum of 12 marks will be available for style and accuracy and a maximum of 13 marks for content and structure.

Here is a list of the criteria used by examiners when assessing your writing. As you can see, they are very detailed but an understanding of their main points will be of help to you in your preparation for the examination. The content and structure section will be revised for each examination to make the points specific to the tasks set. The examiners will balance up the different aspects of each piece of writing and decide which mark best fits it.

Composition tasks: content and structure

Band/ Marks	Argumentative/discursive task	Descriptive task	Narrative task
1 11–13	• There is consistent quality of well developed, logical stages in an overall, at times complex, argument • Each stage is linked to and follows the preceding one and sentences within paragraphs are soundly sequenced	• There are many well defined, well developed ideas and images, describing complex atmospheres with a range of details • Overall structure is provided through devices such as the movements of the writer, the creation of a short time span, or the creation of atmosphere or tension. There is no confusion with writing a story. Repetition is avoided and the sequence of ideas makes the picture clear to the reader	• The narrative is complex and sophisticated and may contain devices such as sub-texts, flashbacks and time lapses. Cogent details are provided where necessary or appropriate • The different sections of the story are carefully balanced and the climax carefully managed. Sentence sequences are sometimes arranged to produce effects such as the building up of tension or providing a sudden turn of events

Band/ Marks	Argumentative/discursive task	Descriptive task	Narrative task
2 9–10	• Each stage of the argument is defined and developed, although the quality of the explanation may not be consistent • The stages follow in a generally cohesive progression. Paragraphs are mostly well sequenced, although some may finish less strongly than they begin	• There is a good selection of interesting ideas and images, with a range of details • These are formed into an overall picture of some clarity, largely consistent. There may be occasional repetition and opportunities for development or the provision of detail may be missed. Sentences are often well sequenced and the description is often effective	• The writing develops some features that are of interest to a reader, although not consistently so. Expect the use of detail and some build-up of character or setting • The writing is orderly and the beginning and ending (where required) are satisfactorily managed. The reader is aware of the climax even if it is not managed fully effectively. The sequencing of sentences provides clarity and engages the reader in events or atmosphere
3 7–8	• There is a series of relevant points and a clear attempt is made to develop some of them. These points are relevant, straightforward and logical/coherent • Repetition is avoided, but the order of the stages in the overall argument can be changed without adverse effect. The sequence of the sentences within paragraphs is satisfactory, although opportunities to link ideas may not be taken	• There is a selection of effective ideas and images that are relevant to the topic and which satisfactorily address the task. An attempt is made to create atmosphere and to provide some details • The description provides a series of points rather than a sense of their being combined to make an overall picture, but some of the ideas are developed successfully, albeit straightforwardly. Some sentences are well sequenced	• A straightforward story (or part of story) with satisfactory identification of features such as character and setting • While opportunities for appropriate development of ideas are sometimes missed, the overall structure is competent, and features of a developed narrative are evident. Sentences are usually sequenced to narrate events
4 5–6	• Mainly relevant points are made and they are developed partially with some brief effectiveness • The overall argument shows signs of structure but may be sounder at the beginning than at the end. There may be some repetition. It is normally possible to follow sequences of ideas, but there may be intrusive ideas or misleading sentences	• Some relevant and effective ideas are provided and occasionally developed a little, perhaps as a narrative. There is a feeling of atmosphere, but most of the writing is of event or description of objects or people • There is some overall structure, but the writing may lack direction and intent. There may be interruptions in the sequence of sentences and/or some lack of clarity	• A relevant response to the topic, but largely a series of events with occasional details of character and setting • The overall structure is sound although there are examples where a particular section is too long or too short. A climax is identified but is not effectively described or led up to. Sentence sequences narrate events and occasionally contain intrusive facts or misleading ideas
5 3–4	• A few relevant points are made and although they are expanded into paragraphs, development is very simple and not always logical • Overall structure lacks a sense of sequencing. Paragraphs used only for obvious divisions. It is sometimes possible to follow sequencing of sentences within paragraphs	• Content is relevant but lacking in scope or variety. Opportunities to provide development and detail are frequently missed • Overall structure, though readily discernible, lacks form and dimension. The reliance on identifying events, objects and/or people sometimes leads to a sequence of sentences without progression	• A simple narrative with a beginning, middle and end (where appropriate). It may consist of simple, everyday happenings or unlikely, unengaging events • Unequal or inappropriate importance is given to the sections of the story. Dialogue that has no function may be used or over-used. There is no real climax. Sentence sequences are used only to link simple series of events

Band/ Marks	Argumentative/discursive task	Descriptive task	Narrative task
6 1–2	• A few points are discernible but any attempt to develop them is very limited • Overall argument only progresses here and there and the sequence of sentences is poor	• Some relevant facts are identified, but the overall picture is unclear and lacks development • There are examples of sequenced sentences, but there is also repetition and muddled ordering	• Stories are very simple and narrate events indiscriminately. Endings are simple and lack effect • The shape of the narrative is unclear; some of the content has no relevance to the plot. Sequences of sentences are sometimes poor, leading to a lack of clarity
– 0	• Rarely relevant, little material, and presented in a disorderly structure. Not sufficient to be placed in Band 6	• Rarely relevant, little material, and presented in a disorderly structure. Not sufficient to be placed in Band 6	• Rarely relevant, little material, and presented in a disorderly structure. Not sufficient to be placed in Band 6

Composition tasks: style and accuracy

Band	Marks	Criteria
1	11–12	• Fluent; variety of well made sentences, including sophisticated complex sentences where appropriate, used to achieve particular effects • Wide, consistently effective range of vocabulary with appropriately used ambitious words • Some use of grammatical devices; assured use of punctuation; spelling accurate
2	9–10	• Mostly fluent; sentences correctly constructed, including a variety of complex sentences • Vocabulary often effective, sometimes complex, mostly varied • Grammatically correct; punctuation mostly correct between and within sentences; very occasional spelling mistakes
3	7–8	• Occasional fluency; sentences of some variety and complexity, correctly constructed • Appropriate and accurate vocabulary with occasional examples of choice made to communicate precise meaning or to give interest • Simple grammatical terms correct; sentence separation mostly correct but other forms of punctuation sometimes inconsistently used; occasional spelling mistakes – but no error of any sort impedes communication
4	5–6	• Sentences tend to be simple and patterns repetitive. Where more complicated structures are attempted there is lack of clarity and inaccuracy • Vocabulary communicates general meaning accurately • Some errors of punctuation including sentence separation; several spelling and grammatical errors, rarely serious
5	3–4	• There may be some straightforward grammatically complex sentences, but others are simple and repetitively joined by *and*, *but*, and *so* with other conjunctions used ineffectively if at all • Vocabulary communicates simple details/facts accurately • Many errors of punctuation, grammar and spelling, but the overall meaning is never in doubt
6	1–2	• Sentences are simple and sometimes faulty and/or rambling sentences obscure meaning • Vocabulary is limited and may be inaccurate • Errors of punctuation, grammar and spelling may be serious enough to impede meaning
	0	• Meaning of the writing is often lost because of poor control of language; errors of punctuation, grammar and spelling too intrusive to award a mark in Band 6

TOPIC 11 Composition tasks in coursework

Summary of coursework requirements

Your coursework portfolio should consist of **three** assignments, each of 500–800 words. These should comprise:

- **Assignment 1** Informative, analytical and/or argumentative writing
- **Assignment 2** Imaginative, descriptive and/or narrative writing
- **Assignment 3** Response to a text or texts chosen by the Centre

Assignments 1 and 2 test continuous writing skills. Assignment 3 tests both reading and writing and will require you to use these skills analytically, as dealt with in earlier sections of this Guide.

Assignments 1 and 2 test the same writing objectives as those tested by Paper 3. To remind you, these are:

- Articulating experience and expressing what is thought, felt and imagined
- Ordering and presenting facts, ideas and opinions
- Understanding and using a range of appropriate vocabulary
- Using language and a register appropriate to audience and context
- Making accurate and effective use of paragraphs, grammatical structures, sentences, punctuation and spelling

The total maximum mark for your coursework portfolio is 50. This comprises a single mark out of 40, for the overall quality of your writing in all three assignments, and a mark out of 10 for reading, which assesses your understanding of the text(s) used in response to the task set for Assignment 3 only. Your teacher will be able to advise you of the criteria used for marking the quality of your work.

Coursework is an alternative to Paper 3 (directed and continuous writing).

The suggestions and practice tasks in Topic 6 (composition skills) of this Guide apply equally to students preparing for the coursework option. However, the following points should be noted.

Key ideas

- Assignments 1 and 2 require different types of writing. Assignment 1 is informative/analytical or argumentative and so requires a more formal register than Assignment 2 which tests imaginative, descriptive or narrative writing.
- It is important that you choose your task carefully in order to suit the demands of each assignment.
- You are in control; you can determine what you are going to write about and how to word the titles of your assignments.
- You should spend some time discussing the task with your teacher and how best to approach it.
- You must include the first draft of **one** of your assignments with your coursework portfolio.
- If you are taking the coursework option, you have time to draft your work and revise it after consultation with your teacher. You also have the opportunity to research suitable material to use in your response to Assignment 1.

- Coursework assignments should be no more than 800 words in length. There is little to be gained by greatly exceeding this limit. Very often, the more you write, the more your limitations are revealed.
- If you word-process your work, it makes revisions easier to do.
- Don't over-revise your coursework assignments. Too much revision can be counter-productive. It should be possible to complete each piece of coursework in the following four stages:
  - **i)** decide on title/topic
  - **ii)** produce an outline plan (to be discussed with your teacher)
  - **iii)** write first draft (hand in to teacher for comments, indications of errors to be corrected and suggestions for improvements)
  - **iv)** final draft, taking note of and incorporating suggestions/ revisions suggested at first draft stage.
- Once you have completed your final draft of each assignment, put it in your portfolio and resist the temptation to tinker with it further. There's always the danger that by doing so you could spoil what is a perfectly good piece of work.
- Debating and discussing ideas, in preparation for an argumentative writing assignment, could also provide practice for a speaking and listening coursework assignment.
- Remember: coursework must be all your own original work. Downloading material from websites and attempting to pass it off as your own is a very serious offence.

TOPIC 12 Speaking and listening

Key objectives

- To introduce the key terms used to define the skills tested in the speaking and listening component of IGCSE First Language English

- To define the key skills/ideas involved in the speaking and listening component of IGCSE First language English

Key definitions

These are the key terms that define what you need to be able to do in order to approach the speaking and listening component of the IGCSE First Language English examination.

Term	Definition
Understand	To grasp the meaning of
Convey	To enable others to understand your meaning
Sequence	To express ideas/opinions in an order
Relevant	Material that is connected to the topic in hand
Appropriate	Way of speaking that is right for the task and audience

Key ideas

Once you understand what the above terms involve you can read the syllabus objectives for your IGCSE course and create a checklist for yourself which sums up the key aims of the IGCSE First Language English speaking and listening component. Here is a possible checklist:

- Can you understand what is said to you in English when detail is used?
- Can you put ideas and opinions in order before you speak?
- Can you put your ideas, opinions and experiences into words so that others can understand you?
- Can you respond relevantly to what you hear, see or read?
- Can you speak in a way that meets the needs of your audience?

Don't panic! You have been building up your experience of these skills since you began speaking and listening.

How are these skills tested in examinations?

IGCSE First Language English tests your proficiency in these skills by setting a variety of tasks, some of which ask you to use more than one skill at a time. These could be:

- an individual activity
- a pair based activity
- a group activity.

The type of speaking and listening tested could be:

- speech/monologue
- role-play
- dialogue.

The purpose of the speaking and listening tasks could be:

- discussion
- argument
- persuasion
- explanation
- description
- analysis.

You should find out whether you are taking a speaking and listening examination or completing coursework. Some possible tasks are:

- You are given a card in advance of being assessed. The card contains a topic about which you will have to give a 3-4 minute speech.
- You are given a card in advance of being assessed. The card contains a topic that you will have to discuss with the examiner and/or other students.
- You are given a card in advance of being assessed. The card contains a role-play that you will have to act out with the examiner and/or other students.
- You are given a visual stimulus in advance of being assessed (such as a photograph or postcard). You will be expected to discuss this with the examiner.
- You are asked to prepare a speech on a topic you feel strongly about. You then deliver this speech to the examiner.
- You are given a topic, some time in advance of being assessed. You prepare ideas and vocabulary in advance and then discuss the topic generally with the examiner.
- In addition you can do coursework tasks which you and your teachers are free to choose and to prepare in advance.

● **Try this**   Copy the table below and see if you can decide which skill(s) each question is testing:

Task	Discussion	Argument	Persuasion	Explanation	Description	Analysis
Give a speech about your hobby						
Act out a dialogue with your partner where you are a customer returning a faulty item to a shop and they are the sales assistant						
Talk to your teacher about a film you have seen recently						
Give a speech in a debate about whether a theme park should be built on unused land in your town						
Working with three others, analyse the meaning of the poem you have been given						
You have been gifted a large sum of money (enough for a holiday, a computer or a racing bicycle). Analyse which item you would buy and say why						

Examiner's tip

▶ You need to be clear which speaking and listening tasks you will be expected to complete. If you are taking the examination, you will be asked to prepare an individual presentation and a paired discussion. If you are taking the coursework option, you will complete three assignments – an individual one, a paired one and a group one.

TOPIC 13 Using speaking and listening skills

Key objectives

- To make sure that you understand what speaking and listening skills are
- To help you to understand the way that speaking and listening tasks are marked by examiners
- To make sure that you understand the common mistakes that students make when tackling speaking and listening tasks
- To revise key strategies for approaching speaking and listening tasks

Key ideas

Speaking requires planning. Before you start speaking you need to:

- consider to whom you are going to be talking
- choose the correct vocabulary for your audience
- choose the correct tone for your audience
- consider the order in which you will make points
- consider the volume, pace and other ways in which you will vary your voice for maximum effect.

Be aware of others involved in the speaking activity. Whilst you are speaking you need to:

- listen carefully so that you can respond to others
- make sure that everyone can understand you
- encourage others to join in.

Common errors

Some students concentrate too much on *what* they say and not enough on *how* they say it. This means that not all marks can be awarded. ■

Some students ignore listening as a skill. This means that not all marks can be awarded. ■

Sample questions and answers

Sample question 1

Your teenage cousin from overseas has come to stay with his family. You are keen that he sees the best of your town but he has only a day to explore. Role-play the conversation between you and your cousin.

> **Examiner's tips**
> ▶ *Everything* you say should be appropriate to the situation and the listener.
> ▶ The best answers will show evidence of planning and consideration.

Student's answer	YOU	Hi, Deepak, it's great to see you again.
	COUSIN	Hi!
	YOU	So what are your plans whilst you're here? Mum tells me you only have a day to look around? That's tough!
	COUSIN	Yeah. It's not long, so I don't want to waste it going to the Tourist Information Office or seeing something boring. Can you give me any tips?
	YOU	Well, I'd need to know what you consider to be boring first!
	COUSIN	I hate museums but Mum and Dad like a bit of culture!
	YOU	Oh, okay. Well, there aren't many museums in town anyway but I think it might be useful to pop into the Town Hall because there's a good display on the history of this area and how it came to be settled in the first place.
	COUSIN	Yes, but I …
	YOU	It isn't boring, honest. It's got buttons to press and a quiz to do. It'll help you to put everything into perspective and it'd only take about 20 minutes.
	COUSIN	Well, okay, maybe we could start there?
	YOU	Yes, that's an excellent idea because then you're right in the middle of town anyway. So, from there I'd go to the old School House and Courts which are virtually next door. There's a really good café in the School House that sells excellent ice creams!
	COUSIN	That sounds more like it … [*The conversation continues*]

Examiner's comments *This is a good answer as the student starts off by ascertaining what 'the cousin' likes and dislikes, which means that everything (s)he goes on to say is appropriate to the audience. The register used is informal but not too casual and the material has obviously been sequenced to provide a 'tour' without too much travelling.*

Sample question 2 You bought a new pair of shoes last weekend but the heel has broken off. Role-play the conversation that you have with the shop assistant when you take them back to the shop.

Student's answer	SHOP ASSISTANT	Next?
	YOU	Yes, me. Er, I bought these here a while ago and they're rubbish.
	SHOP ASSISTANT	I'm sorry to hear that. What's the problem?
	YOU	Just look at them, you idiot.
	SHOP ASSISTANT	Well, I'm afraid that without some more information, such as when you bought them and how they broke, I really can't help.
	YOU	Pardon? I want to see the manager if that's your attitude … [*The conversation continues*]

Examiner's comments *This answer has not got off to a good start as the student has not thought through what (s)he wants and what (s)he needs to make clear at the start. The language used is informal and is not polite. The 'shop assistant' is already antagonised. However, the student has introduced the topic and could still explain the problem.*

Sample question 3 Give a speech to your class about your plans for the forthcoming holiday.

Student's answer Hi, guys. Well, er I, you know, I reckon we, er I will be staying at home this hols. It's er difficult to say exactly. I might go to the beach for a day or so. I might get a job at the shop. My mate who lives in the city said I could go and hang out there. If I get a job I'll earn some dosh and then I can get a motorbike. I'm really keen on the one in the shop at the garage. It's red. I expect you've seen it, haven't you? Hey, Jo, you know the one? ... [*The speech continues*]

Examiner's comments *This is a worrying start as the student is very hesitant and it would be hard to follow because of the short sentences and 'er's. It seems evident that the speech has not been planned and it seems to be going off the point at the end of the extract. The register is very informal and use of slang such as* dosh *(for money) is not really appropriate in an assessed piece.*

How to improve your answers

1 Read the task carefully

It is very important that you read it *slowly* and *carefully* and work out what kind of question you are answering before you start planning. Work out to whom you are going to be speaking and what the purpose of your speaking will be. This will help you to make decisions about register and sequence.

● **Try this** Look at the following example tasks. Who is the audience in each? What is the purpose of the speaking?

1 Imagine that you are at an interview for a part-time job in a local restaurant. Role-play the interview that might take place.
2 There are plans to place a bus stop right outside your front door. You are at a local community meeting. Give a speech offering your opinion of this plan.
3 Your classmates are upset because one student keeps misbehaving and it is getting the whole class into trouble. Role-play a discussion with the student where you offer them some advice.

2 Use the appropriate register

Once you have worked out your audience, think about the appropriate register. Consider the actual words you will use.

● **Try this** Copy and complete the following table.

Informal word	Formal word
pal	
trip	
bike	
class	
	superb
	exceedingly
	superfluous
	irritable

3 Consider the specific skills involved

Once you have worked out what type of speaking is being assessed you should consider the specific skills involved. Some examination boards even have different assessment criteria for different activities.

● **Try this** Using the assessment criteria given below create a checklist of things to remember for each of the three types of activities featured.

Individual activity

Band/Marks	
1 9–10	The student makes full and well-organised use of content; (s)he gives lively delivery sustaining audience interest; (s)he employs a wide range of language devices (e.g. tone, irony, emphasis) accurately and sometimes eloquently.
2 7–8	The student makes sound use of content; her/his delivery may occasionally be stilted, but audience interest is generally maintained; (s)he employs a good range of language devices soundly.
3 5–6	The student makes adequate use of content; her/his delivery is secure but pedestrian ensuring audience attention; language devices are used safely, but perhaps complacently.
4 3–4	Content is thin or perhaps inconsistently used; the student's delivery is not secure, resulting in some loss of audience interest; (s)he makes limited employment of language devices with some inaccuracy.
5 1–2	Content is mostly undeveloped and/or very thin; the student's delivery is weak and the audience is generally lost; (s)he is not able to employ language devices or devices employed with serious error.
6 0	The student fails to meet the above criteria.

Pair-based activity

Band/ Marks	Speaking	Band/ Marks	Listening
1 5	The student extends the subject matter and elicits responses from the listener; (s)he speaks on equal terms with the listener. (S)he employs a wide range of language devices accurately and sometimes eloquently.	**1** 5	The student responds fully to questions and develops prompts; (s)he deals confidently and sometimes enthusiastically with alterations in the direction of the conversation.
2 4	The subject matter is organised and expressed competently; the student attempts to speak on equal terms with the listener but with a varying degree of success. (S)he employs a good range of language devices soundly.	**2** 4	The student responds appropriately and in some detail to questions and prompts; (s)he deals appropriately with most of the alterations in the direction of the conversation.
3 3	The student deals with the subject matter adequately; the listener is generally but not always prominent. Language devices are used safely.	**3** 3	The student responds to questions adequately but deals less effectively with prompts; alterations in the direction of the conversation are occasionally dealt with.
4 2	There is evidence of some sequencing of ideas relating to the subject matter but only inconsistently so; the student accepts that the listener is in full control of the conversation. There is limited employment of language devices with some inaccuracy.	**4** 2	The student provides limited response to the questions and struggles with developing prompts; (s)he tends to maintain the direction of the conversation.

Band/ Marks	Speaking	Band/ Marks	Listening
5 1	Simple facts and ideas are expressed with generally unsuccessful attempts at organisation; the student is barely capable of engaging in a two-way conversation. (S)he is not able to employ language devices or devices employed with serious error.	5 1	The student responds simply or is unable to respond to questions or prompts; (s)he cannot recognise alterations in the direction of the conversation.
6 0	The student fails to meet the above criteria.	6 0	The student fails to meet the above criteria.

Group activity

Band/Marks	
1 9–10	The student can argue ideas and opinions in persuasive detail without dominating the rest of the group; (s)he is adept at acting as group leader; (s)he usefully refers back to previous points; (s)he is always looking to suggest new approaches and to move forward; (s)he listens sympathetically and considers the views of others fully.
2 7–8	The student can argue ideas and opinions soundly but may at times overshadow other members of the group; (s)he is capable of leading the group but with only partial assurance; (s)he refers back to previous points soundly but not entirely successfully; (s)he recognises the need to suggest new approaches but implements this only partially; (s)he listens with a degree of sympathy for others' views but has a tendency to interrupt at times.
3 5–6	Frequent but generally brief contributions are made by the student; (s)he generally accepts a position of group member rather than facilitator/leader; (s)he makes occasional reference to previous points; (s)he may help to support new approaches but rarely initiates them; (s)he listens carefully and responds briefly but appropriately to others.
4 3–4	Brief and infrequent contributions are made by the student; (s)he plays a limited part in the group; (s)he cannot utilise previous points; (s)he follows the general drift of the discussion but struggles to support new approaches; (s)he listens inconsistently and may even drift away from the discussion.
5 1–2	The student may make only one or two contributions or may offer mostly inappropriate contributions; (s)he plays no real role in group membership; is largely ignorant of previous points; does not offer support for new approaches; (s)he may appear to listen but shows little evidence of listening.
6 0	The student fails to meet the above criteria.

4 Plan and structure your material

Practise planning and structuring the material that you will speak about under time pressure. This is really no different from planning an essay. First brainstorm the things that you wish to include in your speaking and then try to put them into a logical order which meets your audience's needs. For example:

Step 1

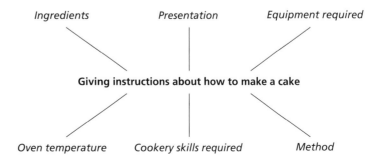

85

Step 2
1 Cookery skills required
2 Equipment required
3 Ingredients
4 Method
5 Oven temperature
6 Presentation

● **Try this**   Practise brainstorming and then sequencing points for a piece of speaking work on the following topics:
  ● A debate on why schools should have uniform
  ● A dialogue about your favourite book
  ● A piece of group work analysing a newspaper report
  ● A role-play where you explain the education system in your country to a visitor from overseas

Key revision points
■ Be alert – listen to the way others speak in different situations, take note of the register that they use and the way they structure their ideas.
■ Be aware – make sure that you know the different skills which go with each type of speaking and listening.
■ Be prepared – practise different types of speaking and listening.
■ Be self-critical – analyse your own strengths and weaknesses by videoing yourself or recording your voice. Then play the recording back and ask yourself whether your voice is clear, interesting and appropriate.

Preparing for the examination

Note that the heading to this section is 'Preparing for the examination' not 'Revising for the examination'. English is different from other subjects as you do not have any facts or theories that you can learn before the exam. The IGCSE First Language English examination requires you to apply what you have learned throughout your years of studying English at school. As this Guide shows you, you will be tested on your ability to read and understand what someone else has written, to express your own ideas in writing and (if you take the option) to communicate with another person or persons by speaking to them and listening to what they have to say.

So, what are the best ways to prepare for an examination in English? Think about the following.

Know what is required

- As part of your preparation you should make a point of becoming familiar with the content of past examination papers and their mark-schemes so that you are aware of exactly what the examiners will be expecting of you. If possible, you should start to do this at the beginning of the school year in which you will take the examination.
- By using this Guide you have already made a start on this process but there are other resources for you to use as well. Your school or college should be able to provide you with details of the most recent IGCSE First Language English specification booklet and examples of past papers for practice, but you can also find this information on the CIE website www.cie.org.uk which also contains copies of the principal examiners' reports on candidates' performance in previous examinations. These are full of good advice about how to approach particular types of questions.
- If possible, try to obtain copies of past papers, the appropriate mark-schemes and principal examiners' reports and then compare your answers to the question papers with the information given in this material. It is helpful if you can do this with a group of friends so that you can discuss matters in detail with each other.
- When you are analysing your response to the question papers, it is important not just whether your answers are right or wrong, but to consider the processes that produce the best answers. What exactly are the examiners looking for? Spend some time thinking about and discussing the wording of questions and how a clear understanding of this can enable you to focus your response on what is specifically required.

Preparing for reading tasks – practise active reading

- You can prepare for the examination by becoming familiar with the type of material that you will be required to read as part of your examination. This will include such things as newspaper and magazine articles as well as fictional and narrative texts. Try to read a selection of these at regular intervals in the months before the examination. In particular, try to read articles in which the writer is presenting an argument for or against a particular point of view.

- Always keep a pencil and piece of paper close to hand as you read. Write down the key points in the writer's argument as you read the article. Don't skip over sections that appear to be difficult to understand; read through them, trying to get an overall understanding of what the writer is saying, and then re-read them, concentrating on the more specific details. It is likely that you will have read similar passages in class, with your teacher asking questions to test your understanding. As you read, think of the sort of questions your teacher would ask and answer them in your mind.

- When you have finished reading the article, write a very brief summary of what it was about, using the notes you have already made. Think about the way the writer has structured the argument and how effective the examples and illustrations are which have been used. Look at the writer's choice of words and phrases. How do they help to persuade you (or otherwise) to agree with the point of view that is being expressed? What would be the effect of choosing different words?

- Taking this approach should help you gain a good understanding of what you have been reading and will prepare you for reading things in a similar way in the examination. However, by analysing the way the writers have expressed themselves, you are also doing something that will help you to improve your writing skills. You could develop this exercise by writing something of your own, such as an article which argues against the points made by the writer in the passage you have been reading.

- The IGCSE First Language English examination tests your reading in different ways and you should practise the techniques required to answer the different tasks successfully. You are being tested on your ability to understand the questions as well as the passage(s) on which they are set. Becoming familiar with how examiners word their questions, by looking at past papers, is a good way to prepare for the examination.

- Some questions will require you to explain what the passage says about something and others will ask you to explain what the writer may be suggesting or how (s)he achieves certain effects. Make sure that your preparation allows you to distinguish between these different approaches so that you can respond appropriately when it matters – in the examination room!

- Your reading skills will also be tested by the summary tasks. Writing a good summary requires a methodical approach both in reading the original passage and in structuring your own response. Your teachers and course books will provide you with suggestions about summary writing techniques but it is important that you practise them so that you are well prepared for the examination. Summary writing is a skill which can be applied to subjects other than English; it is quite likely that History and other subjects will provide you with equal practice opportunities.

- Another way in which your reading is tested is in the directed writing tasks. To prepare for these you should make sure that you are familiar with the conventions of the different formats in which you may be required to write (such as letters, reports, speeches or dialogue) and, in particular, the register which is best suited to each one. However, you should also practise by reading suitable passages in order to select and pick up on relevant details in the text to provide yourself with the information needed to develop your own written response. Again, past papers and this Guide will be of value here.

Preparing for writing tasks

- It is a good idea to become familiar with the requirements of the mark-schemes used by the examiners, see for example pages 73–75.
- For the continuous writing tasks you will be awarded marks both for style and accuracy and for content and structure. For the directed writing you will also be assessed on your skills in applying what you have read.
- The best way to prepare for examination writing tasks is to ensure that you have a good knowledge of your own particular strengths and weaknesses.
- You should practise continuous writing consistently throughout your IGCSE course. Concentrate, in particular, on developing your ideas fully. When your teacher corrects your writing, make sure that you fully understand the errors of expression you have made and how to correct them.
- Build up a log in your own mind of the mistakes you make most frequently and try to avoid making them again.
- When you have finished a piece of writing, read it through carefully. Check, in particular, for these frequently made errors. Whenever possible, try to allow plenty of time between finishing your writing and checking it. When you do check it, try to look on it from the reader's point of view; it is a good idea to get one of your friends to read what you have written (and for you to repay the favour) to check whether everything makes sense.
- Before you sit the examination, you should ensure that you are fully confident about when and where to use the main punctuation devices such as full stops, apostrophes and speech marks. Using these correctly is fundamental to good writing.
- When you are practising writing for the examination, pay particular attention to constructing and linking paragraphs; writing skeleton paragraph plans is helpful and becoming confident in how to vary ways of linking paragraphs is also important.

- Become familiar with the type of writing tasks that are set in the examination and, most importantly, decide on what type of task you are able to do best under examination conditions. You have only one chance in the examination, so it is important that you choose the type of task that will allow you to show your skills to the full.

- The type of writing task that you can do best under examination conditions may not always be your favourite type of writing. For example, you may enjoy writing lengthy short stories but have difficulty in reducing them to something that can be written in less than an hour, so you may find it easier to produce a descriptive task under controlled conditions.

- Examiners will reward the use of a wide and appropriate vocabulary. When you are practising writing for the examination spend some time thinking about and choosing the best words you can to express your ideas; it is important that you develop a wide active vocabulary in order to convey your thoughts as precisely as possible to your readers. Your **active vocabulary** consists of the words you use in your own writing; your **passive vocabulary** consists of the words you recognise when other writers use them. The more you can transfer words from your passive vocabulary to your active one, the better your writing will be.

- Be conscious of the need to express yourself clearly in all of the writing you do, no matter whether it is work you are doing for English lessons, writing up Science experiments or sending e-mails and text messages to your friends. It is important that you reach the stage where you are able to translate the thoughts and ideas in your head directly to words on the page or screen.

- Read as much as you can of all types of writing; make yourself familiar with the ways different writers address different audiences. Try to absorb their sentence structures and turns of phrase into your own writing so that you have a variety of different writing patterns in your head to draw from when it matters.

And finally …

Remember your teachers; they are the people who know your work best and who know what is required to be successful in examinations. Take note of the advice they give you and of the suggestions they make to help you improve and correct your work. Make sure that you ask them to explain anything about which you are not sure before it is too late.

Answers

Topic 2

Student A

1		3 marks
2	i)	2 marks
	ii)	0 marks
	iii)	0 marks
3	i)	1 mark
	ii)	1 mark
	iii)	1 mark
4	i)	2 marks
	ii)	1 mark

Total: 11 marks

Student B

1		3 marks
2	i)	1 mark
	ii)	0 marks
	iii)	0 marks
3	i)	0 marks
	ii)	0 marks
	iii)	1 mark
4	i)	1 mark
	ii)	0 marks

Total: 6 marks

Topic 3

Student C

The answer is very short. Although this student does pick out some of the earlier evidence for the teacher's fear there is not enough. There is no explanation of the effect of the words. This falls into Band 4 as the choice of words is not insecure.

[3 marks]

Student D

This answer is good. The student has picked out a range of words from the whole passage, although there is still more which could have been used. The words and phrases are explained and effects are explored. The writer's objectives are obviously understood which means that the response falls in Band 2.   [8 marks]

Topic 4

Student E

This answer is good. The student uses much of the relevant material and the ideas are developed with some interesting detail. There are positive points made. The piece is well structured with orderly sections of information. Within each paragraph there is progression and the style is persuasive.

[content: 12 marks]
[written expression: 5 marks]

Student F

This answer is not as effective; it is clearly using the material from the text but it is a little mechanical and repetitive. The detail used is not always effective. The piece is structured into a chronological account but there is no other sense of sequence. The persuasion is added on at the end.

[content: 8 marks]
[written expression: 3 marks]

Topic 5
Student G

This answer is very concise and wastes no words

[15 + 5 = 20 marks]

Student H

This answer is too general and often irrelevant

[4 + 1 = 5 marks]

Index